"THERE WERE GIANTS

GLIMPSES OF ROMAN CATHOLIC HISTORY IN CENTRAL MASSACHUSETTS

IN THOSE DAYS!"

Owen J. Murphy Jr.

DIOCESAN MISSION STATEMENT

As individuals, families and parishes,
our mission as the Diocese of Worcester
is to respond joyfully to Christ's call
to become more fully the People of God.

Though imperfect, we are a blessed people
striving to participate in Christ's mission
of reaching out to all. Therefore, we accept
the Gospel challenge, which calls us to bring
another to a deeper knowledge and love of God.

Since God calls us to live in community
in the Holy Spirit, we commit ourselves
in this time and place to becoming a prayerful
and faith-filled Church that truly reflects
the glory of God.

Adopted 1988

AUTHOR:
Owen J. Murphy Jr.

COVER DESIGN:
Juliette Roussel

PUBLISHER:
Éditions du Signe - B. P. 94 - 67038 Strasbourg - France

PUBLISHING DIRECTOR:
Christian Riehl

DESIGN AND LAYOUT:
Juliette Roussel

DIRECTOR OF PUBLICATIONS:
Dr. Claude-Bernard Costecalde

PUBLISHING ASSISTANT:
Sylvie Asimus

COPYRIGHT TEXT:
© Diocese of Worcester, 2000

COPYRIGHT DESIGN AND LAYOUT:
© Éditions du Signe, 2000

ISBN: 2-7468-0192-2
"United States Library of Congress registration and copyright
information is available upon request."Printed in Italy by Stige (Torino)

CONTENTS

"Our Lady at Worcester Center," the gilded statue in the front yard of Notre Dame des Canadiens Church, was saved from the fire that destroyed the first Notre Dame Church and ravaged the surrounding neighborhood in mid-October, 1908.

ABOUT THE COVER:

Looking southwest from the confluence of I-195 and Rte. 2 in northeastern Worcester County, St. Cecilia Church rises like a phoenix from the New England forest, dominating not only the Leominster skyline but the entire Nashoba Valley that eventually gives way to Mount Wachusett in Princeton, the region's highest elevation at 2,006 feet. Established as a parish in January, 1900, St. Cecilia's began construction of its present 1,200-seat church in 1931 — during the depths of the Great Depression — partly as a means of providing employment for parishioners. A lack of funds prevented its completion at that time, but a late-1970s' lightning strike on its 227-feet high steeple — the highest point in the city — spurred new resolve in the Franco-American community to complete what their forebears had begun. When engineers determined that damage inflicted by the lightning bolt had put the entire neo-Gothic structure on Mechanic Street in peril, parishioners surprisingly, but overwhelmingly, opted to bring down the entire edifice and replace it with a less-opulent building. Ultimately, however, less severe sentiment prevailed and the steeple was repaired, the church was completed and a rededication was held in May of 1984. Today, complete with the stained glass windows and statuary the parish could not afford in the 1930s, St. Cecilia's is one of the aesthetic and artistic treasures of the Diocese of Worcester.

Overlaid on the back cover is a map identifying the 60 surviving cities and towns of Worcester County, whose boundaries are identical to those of the diocese.

ACKNOWLEDGMENTS:

Most color photography herein, including the cover photo, is by Frantisek Zvardon. Black-and-white photos, invariably, are from the collection of *The Catholic Free Press*. The Confirmation 2000 photo on Page 6 is by Thomas Keegan, as is the west transept window in St. Paul Cathedral on Page 81. The sketch of St. Augustine Mission, Wheelwright, on Page 120 is copyrighted by Barbara Landry. The photo of Bishops O'Leary and Dinand on Page 141 is from the archival collection of the College of the Holy Cross.

ABOUT THE AUTHOR:

Owen Murphy, a former editor of *The Catholic Free Press*, traces his roots to Ireland through St. Brigid Parish in Millbury, where his paternal great grandparents settled in the middle of the 19th Century, and through St. John Parish in Worcester, where his maternal great grandparents settled, also in mid-19th Century, and where his parents were married.

His children also trace their roots through St. Monica Parish in Coos Bay, Oregon, where their parents were married in 1958 and where their maternal grandparents settled after arriving from Cardeto, a mountain village above Reggio, Calabria, Italy, early in the 20th Century.

THANKS:

To Eleanor for unaffected goodness, unshakable faith — and oh-so-much laughter!

To Bishop Reilly and Father John Bagley for making the pursuit of a "popular diocesan history" a happy journey, and to Father Charles Monroe, Father Michael Rose and William Trainor, Esq., for helping to bring manuscript and illustrations together. To David O'Brien for benevolent counsel.

To Bishop Rueger, the moderator of the diocesan curia, and the staff of *The Catholic Free Press*, and to Mark Savolis and the other custodians of the archival collections at Holy Cross College for uncounted courtesies. To the staffs of the Worcester Historical Museum and the Worcester Public Library's Worcester Room, and to Worcester City Clerk David Rushford and Robert Tivnan in the office of the Worcester County commissioners for welcomed direction.

To Robert Johnson-Lally, archivist of the Archdiocese of Boston, and Father Richard Meehan, archivist of the Diocese of Springfield, for meticulous research and patience, and to parish historians all across the diocese whose collective memory is an incomparable resource.

FOREWORD

March 7, 2000

How appropriate it is that as the universal Church is celebrating the Great Jubilee of the Year 2000 and the Diocese of Worcester is celebrating its Golden Jubilee, this first history of our local Church should be published.

To cherish our roots, to know the struggles and successes of the past, to look back and to realize that "there were giants in those days" are necessary and, indeed, indispensable ingredients to being Church today and for preparing the Church for tomorrow.

How beautifully our roots and past events and great people, clergy, Religious and laity, are presented to us in this volume both as a source of spiritual inspiration and as a reservoir of religious energy.

Surely our history as a diocese and all that preceded and prepared its founding, show us that it was anything but an easy task, but these facts also show us how richly we have been blessed. The common thread of unity and strength that runs thorough this history is that the Church in this diocese has not been wanting for talented clergy, devoted Religous and remarkable laity. I am so grateful that their story is now being told in this special way.

I wish to express my deep appreciation to Mr. Owen J. Murphy Jr., a gifted writer with a great sense of history, who is the author of this work and who brought our history to life in such a readable way. His talent, faith and love of the Church have given a precious gift to our diocese.

I wish also to thank Father John J. Bagley, chairman of our Millennium Celebration Committee, and the members of its history committee for the time and expertise they gave to bring this history into being. The work of choosing the photos that tell the story was primarily their task. We are indebted to them.

Let us be mindful that what we are doing today will be the history of our diocese tomorrow. Let us be faithful to the work and example of our forebears in the faith here in Worcester County and let us always ask the Lord for the help and strength we need to be the "giants" of our day.

✝ Daniel P. Reilly

(Most Rev.) Daniel P. Reilly
Bishop of Worcester

A highlight ceremony of the Jubilee 2000 celebration in the diocese was the confirmation ceremony in Worcester's Centrum on Pentecost Sunday, June 11, 2000, when Bishop Reilly and Bishop Rueger, assisted by diocesan priests, administered the Sacrament of Confirmation to 2,300 young people from parishes throughout the diocese. More than 18,000 relatives and friends thronged the arena and civic center next door for the rite, believed to have been the largest ever held in New England.

REMEMBERING
OLD WORLD WORCESTER

Oh, there had been other great moments in central Massachusetts' history.

After all, even George Washington slept here. Several times.

But it would be difficult to identify a more captivating moment — for Catholics, certainly, but, happily, for the wider community as well — than that on a brisk, but sunny, day a half-century ago when then-Archbishop Richard J. Cushing of Boston handed the crozier, the symbol of episcopal authority, to his brilliant and affable former auxiliary bishop, ceremoniously bringing to life the first Roman Catholic Diocese of Worcester in nearly 400 years.

The date was March 7, 1950, the feast day of the scholarly St. Thomas Aquinas.

The time was exactly 10:38 a.m.

As he reached out his left hand and accepted the shepherd's staff from his friend and mentor, Bishop John J. Wright became, at age 40, the youngest diocesan bishop in the United States and assumed responsibility for the first one-county diocese in American Church history.

Nearly 1,400 invited guests, including one other archbishop, 20 other bishops and abbots and some 700 priests, from Worcester County

and beyond, sat in rapt silence in the newly-designated Cathedral Church of St. Paul and watched the drama unfold. Loudspeakers carried an account of the pageantry that had never before been seen in central Massachusetts to some 1,200 others gathered in the cathedral's lower church and to the more than 15,000 men and women and boys and

TOP OF THE PAGE: Bishop Wright accepts the crozier, the symbol of episcopal authority, from Archbishop Cushing, March 7, 1950.

Bishop Wright, the nation's youngest diocesan bishop on the day of his installation.

Some of the 15,000 people who overflowed Chatham and High Streets on the morning of March 7, 1950.

The Cathedral Church of St. Paul.

girls who thronged the intersection of Chatham and High Streets throughout the emotion-packed morning, their collective body heat and bridled enthusiasm providing an effective defense against the below-freezing chill.

At a later time, without doubt, spontaneous applause would have broken out both inside and outside the stately granite structure in downtown Worcester to acclaim and affirm what was happening in the sanctuary. But more restrained liturgical protocols were in place in those days.

Nonetheless, the excitement that gripped both participants and observers was evident from the moment the 2,500-pound bell that had been installed in St. Paul's long-muted tower only the previous day clapped for the first time to signal the start of the grand procession that emerged from temporary vestries in St. Gabriel Orphanage, St. Paul School and the cathedral rectory. Only the appearance of the genial Archbishop Cushing at the end of the line tested the ability of the platoon of white-gloved Worcester policemen to maintain decorum as he repeatedly reached out to grasp adoring hands en route to the entrance of the church whose dedicatory sermon had been preached a little more than 75 years earlier by the first United States bishop of African-American ancestry.

What followed inside, Thomas J. Sweeney and Philip J. Cogswell reported in an account in Worcester's *Evening Gazette* later in the day, was a ceremony that "fused ecclesiastical elegance and high humility in a gripping pageant governed by ancient formulas still intact."

8

Principals in the March 7, 1950, liturgy.

Vested in a jewel-incrusted miter and cope, Bishop Wright began his new ministry by individually greeting each of the priests entrusted to his care. One-by-one they approached the episcopal throne that, like the new bell in the tower, had been put in place only the previous day, and knelt and kissed his episcopal ring, signifying their obedience to him. The men who took part in that ritual had previously been priests of the Diocese of Springfield but were frozen in one or another of the 60 cities and towns of Worcester County in which they were serving on Jan. 14, 1950, when Pope Pius XII separated those communities from the four counties of western Massachusetts and created the new diocese.

The handsome, canopied throne on which Bishop Wright was seated was not unlike others in Roman Catholic cathedrals all over the world in those days. Indeed, identified by its Latin designation, "cathedra," it was the single piece of ecclesiastical furniture that set a cathedral church apart from other parish churches in any archdiocese or diocese. Not surprisingly, though, given his appreciation of history, the hand-hewn oaken throne that Bishop Wright had commissioned for St. Paul's during the weeks

Cathedral of Worcester, England, which Bishop Reilly planned to visit in October, 2000, in commemoration of the New World diocese's 50th anniversary.

between his appointment as Ordinary and his solemn installation was distinctively and unmistakably Worcester. On either side of the back of the chair itself — symbolically supporting the occupant — were carved representations of St. Oswald and St. Wulstan, two bishops of the nearly-900 year-old diocese of the Old World that was suppressed after the 16th-Century Protestant Reformation reached England, but whose name was now being restored to Church rolls. And carved into its back was the newly-designed coat of arms for the new diocese that includes a cross with fleur-de-lis appendages, recognizing the region's mother church dedicated to the Holy Cross and symbolizing the organization of the Church in New England under Jean Lefevre de Chevrus, a French bishop. Across the top of the shield are

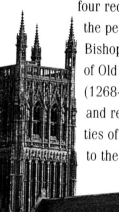

four red discs taken from the personal arms of Bishop Godfrey Giffard of Old World Worcester (1268-1302), recalling and remembering the ties of the new diocese to the old.

Papal Bull establishing the diocese.

Both Archbishop Cushing and Bishop Wright made reference to the reincarnation in remarks during the solemn March 7 liturgy.

In his words of gratitude at the conclusion of the Mass of Installation, Bishop Wright said that "in the happiness of this day…I cannot forget…the saintly bishops, priests and people of Worcester, England, of old who must this day be gratified, even in heaven, that a See bearing the name they love and made glorious, is again inscribed among the militant units which do battle for Christ in communion with Rome."

And in his homily during the Mass, while observing that the new Cathedral Church of St. Paul was "a fair companion" to other cathedrals in Paris, Westminster, Lisbon, Cologne, Madrid, Armagh — even in Rome — Archbishop Cushing observed pointedly: "Canterbury and York have been lost to us — and the Worcester of old — but this Worcester of the New World arises this morning as a cathedral town to perpetuate a name once so glorious in the Church Catholic."

"This morning," Archbishop Cushing told the congregation that included many political, civic and religious leaders not of the Roman Catholic faith, "it is my holy privilege to imitate St. Theodore, archbishop of Canterbury, who, almost 1300 years ago (680) erected the Diocese of ancient Worcester within his jurisdiction. You and I this morning can almost feel the invisible benediction of the great Worcester saints,

Wulstan, the first and the second, and Oswald and Dunstan and the rest."

"The first bishop of the Worcester of the West," Archbishop Cushing said of the man who had been his priest-secretary before being consecrated his auxiliary bishop on June 30, 1947, "(today) takes up a crozier like that laid down by the last bishop of Worcester, Richard Pates, in 1565."

Perhaps there was no reason for the archbishop to mention the contrast in the two events — that Richard Pates had laid down his crozier in exile, caught as he was amid the national upheaval ignited by the lustful King Henry VIII and the discordant convictions of the two heady half-sisters who followed their father and their half-brother to the throne. Richard Pates had been installed as bishop of the Old World diocese in 1555, during the reign of Queen Mary (I), when papal authority was briefly restored to reform-hungry England. He was exiled, however, by Queen Elizabeth (I) who consummated the break with Rome begun some 30 years earlier, and eventually died in Louvain, Belgium, after participating in the counter-Reformation Council of Trent (1545-63).

St. Paul, bathed in sunlight filtered through the windows of the cathedral church.

10

THE CHURCH
ARRIVES IN NEW ENGLAND

It would be sheer speculation to specify when the Mass, whose celebration the Fathers of the Second Vatican Council (1962-65) called "central" to the building up of the Christian community, was first introduced to this magnificent wilderness we call New England.

It could have been in the 6th Century by St. Brendan the Navigator, abbot of Clonfert in County Galway, Ireland — if, that is, his real or storied journeys abroad in the Atlantic took him this far west.

Or it could have been, as Father Edward F. Gully, the first priest ordained specifically for the New World's Diocese of Worcester, speculated in 1975 on the occasion of the silver jubilee of both its establishment and his ordination, John, bishop of Skallholt in Iceland, or Eric, bishop of Gardner in Greenland, each of whom challenged the frigid waters of the North Atlantic into the 12th Century.

It probably wasn't by anyone accompanying Giovanni Caboto, the Genoese who sailed under the English flag — and, consequently, is known to history as John Cabot — because he returned almost immediately after finding a new land mass a bit northeast of what is now the coast of Maine in 1497 to report the discovery to King Henry VII in whose name he had both claimed it and named it — appropriately — "Newefounde Land." Some believe that Caboto eventually did come ashore in Maine on a return journey in 1498-99, before being lost at sea, but evidence of that is not overwhelming.

If a priest were in the company of Miguel Corte Real, a Portuguese sailor who lived among the Wampanoag Indians in Rhode Island after an expedition he was leading was shipwrecked off Block Island in 1502, there is little question that he would have offered the Holy Sacrifice in thanksgiving for the lives spared. Certainly, too, any priest who journeyed with Giovanni Verrazzano, a Florentine in the employ of the king of France, would have offered thanks for the hearty hospitality the crew of their sailing ship received from Native Americans in Newport during the late winter of 1524. Like many other adventurers, Verrazzano and his shipmates had been thwarted by America's eastern coastline in their attempt to find a passageway to the spice-rich Orient, but upon their chance arrival at Narragansett Bay they were welcomed by a veritable flotilla of canoes whose occupants hosted them for several weeks before sending them off in the direction of the Grand Banks and home.

What is undeniable is that sometime early in July, 1604, Father Nicholas Aubry, a Parisian who was a member of an expedition led by Pierre du Guast, Sieur de Monts, celebrated Mass in the far northeastern reaches of what today is the State of Maine.

De Monts and his party, which included Samuel de Champlain, a young French cartographer, held a charter from France's King Henry IV to establish the first permanent European settlement in this part of the New World. "Acadie," as the territory was called, stretched, roughly, from the St. Lawrence River Valley that another Frenchman, Jacques Cartier, had discovered several decades earlier and that Champlain had visited with a trading expedition in 1603, to islands that Giovanni

The icon of the patron of England that graces the Shrine of the Word in St. George Church, Worcester.

Verrazzano and the crew of his "Dauphine" had observed in what today are recognized as Long Island Sound and Nantucket Sound. They first reached landfall in modern-day Nova Scotia in early-May of 1604, but rested there for only a few days before resuming their journey westward, ultimately deciding to settle on an island in what came to be known as Passamaquoddy Bay near modern-day Calais, Maine.

It was there, in keeping with Roman Catholic custom, that the settlers planted a cross, claiming all the territory described in their charter in the name of the French king, and where, after enough of the forest had been harvested to build a rude chapel, Father Aubry began the regular celebration of Mass.

The name the French settlers gave to their island has changed over the intervening years, but the river surrounding it is still known by the

"... this magnificent wilderness we call New England."

North American Martyrs Church, Auburn, constructed on the site of a Native American Village at the "Hill of Pleasant Springs."

St. Joseph Chapel at the College of the Holy Cross.

sacred designation given to both, "Ste. Croix," a name later adopted in its English translation by New England's first Roman Catholic cathedral and by its first Roman Catholic college: "Holy Cross."

De Monts' colonists made good progress during their first summer and autumn in organizing the settlement, but none could imagine the terrible toll the months of winter would take. So devastating were the biting cold and the maladies that accompanied it, however, that when the spring of 1605 did mercifully arrive, more than one-half of the settlers — including young Father Aubry — were dead and plans were immediately set in motion to abandon the place.

Among those who survived the horrific winter was the intrepid Samuel de Champlain who set out shortly thereafter to complete the royal commission he held to chart the hills and valleys and the rugged coastline of all of "Acadie." Sometime in early-July, 1605 — a full 15 years before the Pilgrims stepped onto Plymouth Rock — he reached the territory's southern boundary on Cape Cod and, as if to punctuate the claim of his Catholic patron to every tree, to every blade of grass, to every grain of sand in the region, planted another cross. Yet, when asked to lead the resettlement of New France three years later, Champlain opted not for New England but a site in the St. Lawrence River basin, in the northern extremity of the territory, up river from Montreal near what would become Quebec City.

As it turned out, that decision may have been providential, because after their arrival in Jamestown in 1607, the English colonists who settled Virginia were not timid about making forays up and down the coast to harass any unwelcome visitors they might find. Sailing north from Jamestown, for example, English men-of-war rained cannon fire on the few other English Catholics who had fled from their native land and inadvertently settled on an island off the

The Diocese of Worcester's Millennium Cross.

13

coast of Portland, and on French Jesuits associated with others in Champlain's Canadian colony who had begun ministering to Native Americans near modern-day Bar Harbor in Maine's Mount Desert region.

As a result of those bombardments, every European village in what would later become New England — all of them Catholic at the time — was abandoned from about mid-May of 1613, until that eventful autumn of 1620 when the Mayflower dropped anchor in Cape Cod Bay.

It was in this period that the fundamental contradiction in early-American life became apparent. For while the Anglicans who settled in Virginia and the Pilgrims and Puritans who followed them, into Massachusetts, said they were fleeing to these shores to gain religious freedom, it was a privilege they claimed only for themselves. It wasn't until the onset of the American Revolution a century and one-half later that political necessity — in the form of patriot alliances with Catholic France and Catholic Spain — translated into some semblance of religious toleration. Until then the 13 colonies of English-speaking America were, with only rare and wonderful exception, avowedly Protestant and openly anti-Catholic. And none was more virulent than Massachusetts!

THE BATTLE
CRY OF "NO POPERY"

Settlers of New France continued to be profoundly Catholic, of course. But until that alliance between the colonies and the French was forged in the revolt against the mutually-loathed British, the French presence north of the border in Canada and beyond the Appalachian Mountains in unexplored America only heightened anxiety concerning the spread of Romanism on the continent. And the friendship the French settlers had nurtured with Native American warriors only exacerbated the enmity Protestant-America already harbored toward "papists."

The American Revolution did not eliminate what Irish-born Bishop John England of Charleston (S.C.), the first great apologist of the Catholic Faith in the United States, characterized, early in the 19th Century, as "the hatred of and, in some cases, the deadly hostility toward Catholics in the land." In fact, as the American Protective Association, the Know-Nothing Movement and the Ku Klux Klan of later years would demonstrate, suspicion of Catholics and Catholicism perdured in the United States right up through the end of World War II, perhaps even beyond, if the presidential candidacy of John F. Kennedy in 1960 is a barometer.

St. Cecilia Church, Leominster.

Bishop Wright visits the chicken barbecue pit during the 1952 Lord's Acre Corn Festival of the then-St. Francis Xavier Mission, Bolton, with the then-U.S. Rep. John F. Kennedy who was in his first campaign for a U.S. Senate seat. At right is John P. McGrail, a Berlin resident. Partly hidden by the future President is Rev. John M. O'Brien, then-pastor of the mother parish, Immaculate Conception, Lancaster.

Father Peter Guilday, a professor of Church history at The Catholic University of America, assessed the matter during the presidential campaign of New York Gov. Alfred E. Smith in 1928. Simply put, Father Guilday said what came to be known as "The Catholic Question" was "a legacy of (the) distrust and misunderstanding bequeathed to all those who have descended from, or who have been influenced by, the colonial Puritanism of New England." New England Puritanism had a variety of forms but "recognized a common enemy in the Catholic Church," Father Guilday explained in a series of essays published in *The Catholic Mirror,* the monthly magazine of the Diocese of Springfield, during that tumultuous campaign year.

Throughout the colonial period, he wrote, "the feeling against Catholics never relaxed its vigilance and…was fed by an increasing series of attacks upon 'Popery' in and out of the pulpit." Under the guise of a law against idolatry, Father Guilday reminded his readers, "the celebration of the Mass in Massachusetts was made punishable by death." And by decree of the Massachusetts General Court effective on Sept. 10, 1700, the presence of "Jesuits, priests and Popish missionaries" was forbidden in the territory under penalty of perpetual imprisonment or, if recapture followed a successful escape, death. That law differed from one passed in May of 1647 only in the fact that the earlier statute sanctioned no more than "banishment" for the first offense.

"The deep Puritan horror" of all things savoring of Catholicism, Father Guilday wrote, made even the celebration of Christmas a punishable act. To illustrate Puritan paranoia, the priest-historian

St. Francis Xavier Church, Bolton, constructed in the form of a corn crib to honor the surrounding farmland.

pointed out that fully two-thirds of the titles listed in a catalogue of books and pamphlets published up to the American Revolution were filled with what Sanford H. Cobb called, in his *Rise of Religious Liberty in America,* "the insane cry of 'No Popery'."

Interior of Sacred Heart Church, Webster

its beginnings when a former bishop of Old World Worcester refused to grant the annulment of the marriage of King Henry VIII and Catherine of Aragon, thereby triggering events that culminated in the English Reformation. And, of course, the changes it wrought in both Church and society not only inundated the realm, but, in time, spilled across the Atlantic and saturated life in the American colonies.

"Not to understand the 'No Popery' of the colonial epoch of our history (1607-1776)," Father Guilday maintained in one of his essays during the months of that 1928 presidential campaign, "is to miss completely one of the main elements of the religious life of modern America, even though," he added pensively, "most accounts of American history ignore it."

That aspect of early-Americana should have a particular fascination for Roman Catholics of modern-day central Massachusetts, because the "horror" about which Father Guilday wrote had

It is possible that Henry VIII thought his 1527 petition to Pope Clement VII for release from his marriage to the former Spanish princess so that he could marry the enticing Anne Boleyn would be granted hastily and without question. After all, before his election to the papacy, Pope Clement had been Cardinal Giulio de' Medici, the bishop of Worcester and the guardian of the English king's interests in Rome.

Interior and exterior views of Our Lady of the Rosary Church, Gardner.

Not so, however, and the inevitability of schism became evident.

Ironically, Henry took the first tentative steps toward the break with Rome only seven years after Pope Leo X had granted him the title of "Defender of the Faith" for the diplomatic support he had given the Holy Father and for the vigorous attack he had mounted on Martin Luther and Church reformers on the European continent. When the break was complete, Henry and the offspring who followed him to the throne had clearly outlined the structure of a national church, albeit one that retained many of the teachings and trappings of the Church of Rome. But it was those reminders of Rome that angered the people who wanted ritual and hierarchy purged from their religious lives and gave birth to separatist sects that decried, just as vigorously, the religious uniformity the new Anglican Church was demanding.

Church of St. Thomas-a-Becket, South Barre.

The separatists who came to America as Pilgrims at Plymouth and, a few years later, as Puritans who settled in the region near Cape Ann, also shared a common belief, as Father Gustave Weigel phrased it in his

St. Richard of Chichester Church, Sterling, in the heart of Johnny Appleseed's Nashoba Valley.

1961 volume, *Churches in North America*, "in the necessity of a life of strenuous virtue and simplicity." Not surprisingly, then, by the middle of the 17th Century both groups had joined together to form what they called the Congregational Churches, an affiliation of largely-independent religious congregations whose theology was of the European Protestant school. Their organizational structure was decentralized, but the Congregationalists, as the members came to be known, were intent upon putting into practice the belief of the French reformer, John Calvin, that religious people should not hesitate to organize civic communities that embody their own understanding of God's will.

Church of St. Edward the Confessor, Westminster.

With Calvin, as Father Weigel, a distinguished Jesuit ecumenist, explained it, the Congregationalists believed that "in civil affairs God's people arranged the laws, and no one not of God's people could have a voice. Members of the Church had civil power and no one else. The function of civil government was to order public life in accord with the Gospel as understood by the congregations. And in such a system," Father Weigel wrote, "civil tolerance was out of the question. Non-Christians and Christians of most other denominations were persecuted. Civil government sought out and punished witches. Sobriety and virtue became demands of civil law and the sanctity of the Sabbath (Sunday) was legally imposed."

"These," Father Weigel said prosaically, "were the original Blue Laws."

It was clearly contradictory, but the exclusory tenet of the Congregational Churches — like many of the other laws of colonial America — mirrored the oppressive statutes under which the Anglican Church was flourishing in Mother England. And those, of course, were laws from which the Pilgrims and Puritans claimed to have fled across the Atlantic. Nonetheless, they were the laws that ordered life in colonial Massachusetts.

Classic New England: the First Congregational Church on Shrewsbury Common.

EARLIEST
CATHOLIC ARRIVALS

There is little question that a few Roman Catholics had embraced the serenity of central Massachusetts before the mid-1820s when the vanguard of the Irish contractors, tradesmen and laborers began arriving to build the Blackstone Canal that would link entrepreneurial Worcester and the mill villages of the Blackstone Valley to the markets of the world through Narragansett Bay at Providence.

Among them were French-speaking Acadians, descendants of the pioneers who had abandoned Ste. Croix Island in 1605 and eventually settled across the Bay of Fundy in Nova Scotia. All of the Maritime Provinces in the far western Atlantic had come under British domination by 1714 and, not surprisingly, all the settlers there were expected to pledge their allegiance to the British crown. While the Acadians refused to do so, for some unexplained reason they were allowed to continue their placid — and Catholic — way of life virtually unmolested for more than a half-century. But in 1755, after the almost-continuous wars between the French and the British on the North American continent erupted anew as the French and Indian War (1754-1763), it was determined that the threat the still-defiant Acadian-French posed to English expansion could no longer be tolerated and the order was given for their removal from their adopted homeland.

A force of some 2,000 conscripted soldiers from Massachusetts — including a detachment of 105 men from Worcester County commanded by Capt. Abijah Willard of Lancaster — secretly sailed into Nova Scotia early in September of 1755 and, after sacking and burning the Acadians' farms and villages, escorted virtually the entire population to ships that would take them back to Europe or disperse them throughout the American colonies. Massachusetts received

Notre Dame Church, Southbridge. The exteriors of parish buildings are faced with marble bricks cut from an oversupply of tombstones, thankfully, not needed during the Spanish-American War.

19

The church of the Brookfields' mother parish, St. Joseph's in North Brookfield.

Sacred Heart Church in West Brookfield whose walls had to be reinforced after it suffered severe damage in the horrific Hurricane of 1938.

1,000 of the more than 7,000 exiles, including two families and an unescorted teen-age girl who were settled in Worcester as wards of the county selectmen. Their presence is especially noteworthy because not long after their arrival, the wife of Justin White gave birth to their third child, a baby believed to be the first born of Catholic parents in Worcester County.

There are indications of the presence of a few other Roman Catholics in Worcester County — at least of several people "with Catholic-sounding names" — prior to the Acadians' arrival. Among them was Peter Larkin, later "of French and Indian War fame," as Peter J. O'Toole describes him in a 1949 history commemorating the centenary of the first Catholic church constructed in Clinton. He was "the first Irish settler in the section" when he took up residence in Berlin in 1716, Mr. O'Toole recounted, while also acknowledging that his "descendants were not brought up in the Catholic faith."

Several of the children who were kidnapped by Native American warriors during the 18th Century and taken to villages near Montreal where they were baptized in the Catholic faith, also maintained contact with the region. Historical accounts differ about whether any of the young people ever returned to take up permanent residence hereabouts. But in their (1934) *Story of Worcester*, Albert Farnsworth and George B. O'Flynn, maintain that the oldest daughter of Digory Sergent and his wife, did return to marry and live in the homestead on the eastern slope of Worcester's Union Hill where her father was killed by a hostile force in 1702 and from where she, her mother and her four brothers and sisters had been

St. Luke the Evangelist Church, Westboro. Badly damaged in the 1953 tornado, it is the successor of two earlier churches that burned to the ground.

abducted. The children's mother died in the hills beyond Tatnuck just as their perilous journey north was getting underway, but the youngsters, like most of the other children taken captive from Worcester County during that era, survived and were instructed in the Catholic faith and baptized by French Jesuits ministering in the Indian villages along the St. Lawrence River.

Father John J. McCoy, the chronicler of the early history of the Diocese of Springfield, claimed that Timothy Rice, one of four boys taken captive in 1704 in a raid on Westboro, returned there in 1740 as "a famous chieftain among the Indians." He and a companion, Father McCoy wrote, "were the first two Catholics known to have been in Westboro." The priest-historian also pointed out that "in 1706, at Brookfield, the Indians killed John Cleary" and that in the party of men ambushed by Indian warriors at Wickaboag Pond in the Brookfields in 1675, during King Philip's War, "we find the names of Timothy Farley and John (Mc)Coye." Like many of the militiamen who left from central Massachusetts villages and towns on April 19, 1775, to join the embattled farmers at the Concord Bridge and on the Lexington Green, the Brookfield men, Father McCoy observed, "were unquestionably Irish (although) we cannot now make proof that they were Catholics."

What is certain is that any Catholics who did settle in the Province of Massachusetts prior to the American Revolution practiced their faith anonymously and with neither churches nor clergy — excepting, of course, on those occasions when a courageous priest might have clandestinely attended them. The commonwealth, as events unfolded, would not know a resident Catholic priest until 1788 — the year the United States' federal Constitution was ratified — when 37 year-old Abbé Claudius Florent Bouchard de la Poterie, a former French Navy chaplain, settled in Boston. The French fleet was said to have been seeking refuge from hurricanes when it dropped anchor in Boston's harbor in late-summer that year. But when, at last, it set sail again, Abbé de la Poterie

remained ashore, intent upon organizing the Olde Towne's first Catholic parish around an abandoned Huguenot church on School Street that was made available for Catholic use. Whether or not he was a military deserter, as some accounts maintain, it was the abbé who, on Nov. 2, 1788, celebrated therein what Father John E. Sexton said in the (1944) history of the Archdiocese of Boston "may properly be called the first public Mass in Boston."

By that time religious liberty had arrived in Massachusetts, even though the state constitution that was ratified in 1780 continued, for all practical purposes, to block the right of Catholics to hold any public office and continued the tax "for the support and maintenance of public Protestant teachers of piety, religion and morality." But pressure brought by other states in the embryo Republic caused the Massachusetts constitution also to proclaim that:

"No subject shall be hurt, molested, or restrained in his person, liberty, or estate for worshiping God in the manner and season most agreeable to

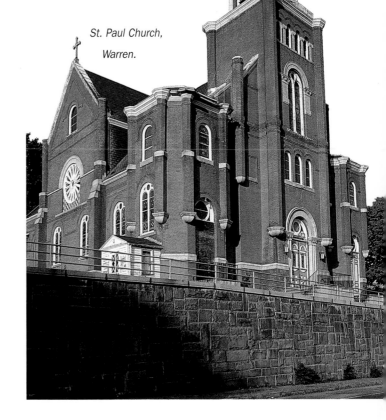

St. Paul Church, Warren.

21

the dictates of his own conscience, or for his religious profession or sentiments."

Fittingly, the people whom Abbé de la Poterie gathered together for worship on School Street dedicated their little brick church to the memory of the ill-fated pioneer settlement on the Ste. Croix River that a cruel winter had ravaged almost two centuries earlier. Fittingly, too, that congregation matured into the parish of New England's mother church — Boston's Holy Cross Cathedral — where the relic of the True Cross of Jesus Christ that Abbé de la Poterie possessed and exposed for veneration following the first Mass, is still preserved.

Nearly another half-century would pass before Worcester County would have its first permanent Catholic church or its first resident Catholic priest, but in the meantime, the Church would be taking firm root throughout the new nation.

St. Stanislaus Church, West Warren.

CORNERSTONE
WELL SET

Whatever Catholics there were in the colonies before the American Revolution undoubtedly came under the ecclesiastical jurisdiction of the vicars apostolic of England's London District, even though the extent of their authority was not clearly defined. After the Revolution, the two dozen-or-so Catholic priests living in the former colonies had little inclination to continue any relationship with a bishop residing in England. Further, such an arrangement, however vague, became both impractical and unnecessary when Congress made clear it had no intention of legislating on matters concerning religion. As a result, with the tacit support of Benjamin Franklin, at the time America's

commissioner in Catholic France, the American priests petitioned Church authorities in Rome for the appointment — from among their number — of a vicar apostolic for the United States.

The priests knew such posts were normally filled by bishops, but fearing a resurgence of overt anti-Catholic activity should any bishop — foreign or domestic — be named the immediate superior of the Church in the new Republic, the priests specifically requested the appointment of a priest. After all, even in those places in colonial America where the Anglican Church had been planted there was no general acceptance of an Anglican hierarchy.

Pope Pius VI obviously took the priests' concern to heart because on June 6, 1784, he confirmed 49 year-old Father John Carroll of Maryland as "superior of the mission" in the 13 United States, an office equivalent under Church law to that of vicar apostolic. The choice was a popular one, certainly among the Catholic clergy, but also in the general population that was well aware of the patriot fervor that had energized the Carroll family. It was widely known, for example, that despite his passionate belief that priests should not become involved in political matters, Father Carroll had accepted an invitation from the Continental Congress to accompany a diplomatic mission sent to Canada early in 1776 to negotiate an alliance between the North American neighbors against Britain. And, of course, his cousin, Charles Carroll of Carrollton, a member of the Maryland delegation to the Continental Congress, was the only Catholic to sign the Declaration of Independence. Later, Father Carroll's brother, Daniel, an active and outspoken patriot partisan from the beginning of the revolt, was one of only two Catholics at the Constitutional Convention that, in 1787, debated, framed and ultimately endorsed the United States Constitution.

It was about the time the Constitution was being debated that both the "superior of the mission" and his brother-priests came to realize that if the Church in the new nation were to prosper, it needed a bishop at its head who could exercise personal and not delegated authority. Without doubt the tenor of the debate in Philadelphia also gave them

Archbishop John Carroll, the nation's first Catholic bishop.

confidence that the nation was ready to accept such a personage. Accordingly, they asked the Holy See to name a bishop to shepherd the Church in the United States. Rome responded with equal confidence by inviting the American clergy to gather together and to not only nominate a bishop but also to designate his See City. They did. And on March 25, 1789 — just about five weeks before George Washington was to be inaugurated as the nation's first President — they, in fact, elected, by a vote of 24-to-two, Father John Carroll to the office of bishop. While he would have ecclesiastical jurisdiction over a land mass that stretched from British Canada to Spanish Florida and from the Atlantic Ocean to the Mississippi River — the priests selected Baltimore as the seat of the nation's first diocese because nearly two-thirds of the estimated 25,000 Catholics then living in the vast territory and nearly three-quarters of the priests then serving it resided in Maryland. Pope Pius VI confirmed both selections, effective Nov. 6, 1789.

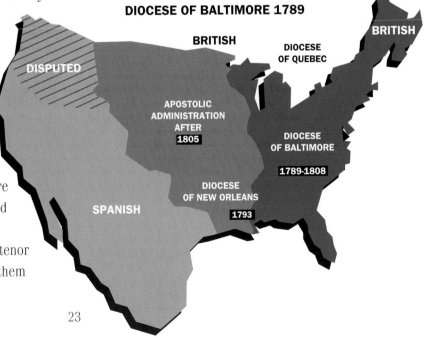

DIOCESE OF BALTIMORE 1789

BRITISH

BRITISH

DISPUTED

DIOCESE OF QUEBEC

APOSTOLIC ADMINISTRATION AFTER 1805

DIOCESE OF BALTIMORE

1789-1808

DIOCESE OF NEW ORLEANS

1793

SPANISH

Our Lady of the Assumption Church, Millbury.

Born in Maryland in 1735, John Carroll was the fourth of seven children of an Irish immigrant father and a mother whose roots went deep into the soil of the only American colony founded by Catholics. Much of his early education was received in France where, in 1753, he entered the Society of Jesus and where, in 1769, he was ordained a Jesuit priest. Upon his return to Maryland in 1774, he became a model of reassurance to those who were bringing the time of tyranny against Catholics on the continent to an end, because his dual loyalties were unabashed. As Annabelle M. Mellville wrote in *John Carroll of Baltimore,* her (1955) biography of the man:

"Never, as priest, superior of the mission, bishop or archbishop did John Carroll ever deviate from (his) conviction that while in affairs spiritual he was always a true son of Rome, in concerns temporal and political he was first and last an American."

Window of the Assumption,
Our Lady Immaculate Church, Athol.

The cornerstone of Catholicism in America was well set, although nearly another year would go by before Bishop-elect Carroll was consecrated. But that happy event, simple though it was, finally took place on Aug. 15, 1790, the Feast of the Assumption of Our Lady, in a chapel about 120 miles southwest of London. Significantly, the site chosen — the chapel at Lulworth Castle in Dorset on the English Channel — became the first post-Reformation Roman Catholic house of worship in Britain when authorities granted permission for it to reopen two years earlier.

Even before receiving full episcopal powers Father Carroll had fences to mend. Among the most in need of attention was the situation in Boston where what were categorized as "tactless improprieties" uttered by Abbé de la Poterie against the French consul escalated into a threat of schism. The antagonisms the abbé's behavior aroused were of such magnitude that Father Carroll was forced to withdraw the Boston

Marquetries (wood inlaid mosaics) in Christ the King Church, Worcester, depicting Old Testament prophets, Isaiah and Daniel.
They, and representations of the 16 other Old Testament prophets, are duplicates of marquetries that adorn the choir stalls in the
Basilica of Sacré Cœur in Paris, France.

priest's faculties to preach and administer the Sacraments — an action that motivated the abbé to besiege Rome with "calumnious correspondence" concerning his superior.

Father Sexton recorded in the section of the archdiocesan history he authored that when that rift was resolved with Abbé de la Poterie's departure for Quebec, the papal nuncio to Paris, "while deeply affected at the scandal...viewed it, nevertheless, as one of 'those storms which the Providence of God, from time to time, permits to reanimate the zeal and the vigilance of the Pilots'." Unfortunately, the storms were not over. In fact, a more serious one that divided the 100-member Boston Catholic community along nationality lines developed almost immediately, demanding that the newly-consecrated Bishop Carroll put a pastoral journey to Boston among his early priorities.

The three-week visit that ran from mid-May to early-June of 1791 was the first by a Catholic bishop to Massachusetts, but given the enmity toward Catholics that heretofore had existed in the commonwealth, the warmth of the reception accorded the bishop by both civic and religious leaders was disarming. He moved easily and graciously among all elements of Boston society. Sadly, however, he was unable to salve the hurts within the congregation he hoped to console.

Bishop Carroll was comfortable in withdrawing the faculties to preach and to teach from Father Louis de Rousselet, Abbé de la Poterie's immediate successor at the School Street church. But installing Father John Thayer as his successor was done without great enthusiasm.

Father Thayer should have been an ideal choice to lead the community because he was not only the first New Englander ordained to the Roman Catholic priesthood, but he was a native Bostonian who had a unique understanding of his environment — having earlier been a Congregational minister. In fact, before what has been called "a thirst for religious enlightenment" led him to a lengthy visit to Europe, Rev. Mr. Thayer had been chaplain to Gov. John Hancock — who, incidentally, was the largest landowner in Worcester during the Revolutionary period. It was during that European sojourn that Rev. Mr. Thayer embraced Catholicism and where, in 1787, following theological studies in France, he was ordained a priest. Bishop Carroll lamented, however, that the young man lacked "amiable conciliatory manners," a personality trait that would have been invaluable in reconciling the French and Irish factions in the tiny Catholic congregation in Boston. As events unfolded it became apparent that the bishop's misgivings were not ill-conceived because within only a few weeks of Father Thayer's appointment as pastor, nearly one-half the community — Irish members as well

Father Francis A. Matignon

as French — was refusing to take part in services he conducted, a fact amply recorded in the public press.

Providentially, within the year Father Francis A. Matignon, a professor of theology and Scripture whom various observers have described as "saintly… tactful… gentle… zealous… prudent" — not to mention "humble" — set sail from France for Baltimore and an eventual assignment by Bishop Carroll to Boston. Archdiocesan historians have acclaimed his arrival in the Hub on Aug. 20, 1792, as the beginning of "a new era…in the history of Boston and New England Catholicity."

Because New England's Catholic roots are part of the anchor of the Church throughout the United States, it is interesting to recall the roles played by Father Matignon and the three other priests who were his shipmates in the arduous 10-week journey they made across the Atlantic in their flight from the anti-clericalism of the French Revolution. Later generations might dispute the claim, but Annabelle Melville's observation in her biography of John Carroll that "four more valuable men to the Church in the United States probably never traveled together" could hardly have been debated when the Church in the United States was aborning. History tells us that Father Ambrose Maréchal became a successor of Archbishop Carroll as archbishop of Baltimore; that Father Gabriel Richard became a circuit-riding missionary in the Midwest and, among other things, founded the University of Michigan and, with ecclesiastical authorization, was the first priest to run for and be elected to the United States Congress; that Father François Ciquart became both a minister to and an advocate for Native Americans in Maine and that Father Matignon, as Dr. Melville put it, "brought lasting peace to the troubled Boston congregation."

Church of Jesus Christ, the King, Worcester.

THE CHURCH SETS ROOTS
IN CENTRAL MASSACHUSETTS

The beginnings of the Church in central Massachusetts, although not nearly as well-documented as at the port of entry in Boston, were far more tranquil. Certainly antagonisms, stirred most often by cultural differences, developed among the Catholic immigrants and strained relationships between them and settlers of long-standing. But any expressions of hostility, from whatever the source, were more often than not neutralized by concurrent acts of kindness, sometimes even of friendship.

The Blackstone Canal as seen in South Grafton.

The first Catholics to take up residence in any great numbers in the central precincts of the commonwealth were the Irish workers who began moving into the valley towns of southern Worcester County in 1825 as work on the Blackstone Canal reached north from Rhode Island into Massachusetts. The 46-mile-long Blackstone River was already recognized, of course, as the place where the Industrial Revolution had been introduced to

America 30-plus years earlier. In time, primarily because of the power its cascading waters would provide for the scores of mills and factories that sprouted along its banks, the Blackstone would be given the accolade: "America's hardest working river." But when the first earth was dredged in Providence in 1824, initiating the canal project, it also promised to be navigable for barge traffic — all the way to Worcester.

Many of the earliest Irish arrivals to valley towns were common laborers, but others were highly-skilled tradesmen experienced in the design and construction of the locks that would be necessary to ease the canal barges up or down the 451-feet elevation between central Massachusetts and the sea. Most of the skilled workers had mastered their trade in so-called "navigation projects" all across England before sailing for America to work on the fabled Erie Canal that cut across New York State and blended the waters of the Great Lakes with

Canal machinery and equipment shed still in existence that were undoubtedly fashioned by Catholic laborers.

those of the Hudson River and the port of New York. When work on that massive project began winding down around 1824, several Irish contractors, including Tobias Boland, a founder of historic Christ Church in Worcester a few years later, transported many of their best people from New York to work on the Blackstone Canal that would open that romantic, if brief, period when Worcester was a seacoast town.

The skills and strong backs of the "Irishies," as Yankee residents called the canal workers, were naturally welcomed by those who recognized the great transportation and communication resource the waterway would be.

But their persons were not.

The men were as unwelcome in the valley villages as were the first of their number who arrived in Worcester in 1826 to begin constructing the canal's northern terminus. Fear of the foreigners was so great that when they were not on the construction site, they were invariably required to stay in the camps that had been set up for them away from the town centers. Even greater, however, was a gnawing foreboding among the settled folk that once the canal project was finished, some of the workers might be tempted to take up permanent residence.

William Lincoln, a member of, perhaps, the era's most prominent Worcester family and a representative of the town on the Blackstone Canal Co., did his best to assure his fellow-citizens that "the Irish are coming to build the canal, not to live here." Alas, even he did not foresee the other employment opportunities the completed canal would immediately inspire — on and off the water — when freight needed to be hauled, barges needed to be manned, warehouses needed to be built, stables needed to be tended, roads and sidewalks needed to be laid out. Certainly Mr. Lincoln didn't anticipate the manpower needs of railroad builders so soon after the canal's completion, much less that the agonizing work of blasting ledge and leveling hills and building bridges and laying tracks would forever change the social composition as well as the physical landscape of virtually every community in Worcester County.

But when all of that did happen and the "Irishies" began to settle into Worcester's and Worcester County's first ethnic neighborhoods, among their most cherished friends was William Lincoln.

The U.S. Arms Hotel and the North Main Street marker calling attention to a Mass said to have been celebrated there by Bishop Fenwick.

When the first of the Church's ministers traveled to central Massachusetts to celebrate Mass or the Sacraments with the new settlers is unclear, even though later arrivals have long endorsed what a sidewalk marker on North Main Street in Worcester proclaims:

"In the year 1826 the Holy Sacrifice of the Mass was offered for the first time in Worcester by the Rt. Rev. Benedict Fenwick in a room in the United States Arms Tavern which stood on this site."

That Mass, which local lore also has maintained was the first to be offered in Worcester County, was believed to have been a devotional, or private, Mass probably celebrated by the revered bishop in one of the small dining rooms of the popular hostelry.

There is little doubt that such a Mass by such a personage would have been an event significant enough to warrant eventual commemoration on a bronze plaque. After all, just before the invasion by several hundred canal builders during the summer of that year (1826) Worcester was, as Albert B. Southwick, a Leicester-born journalist and historian, has described it, "a small,

isolated, inbred town" whose population of about 3,000 had "only 19 foreign-born persons" and "no Roman Catholics."

But no documentation survives to authenticate the Mass. Indeed, every indication is that at least two years more would pass before a Catholic priest would visit the region and that nearly six years would pass before Bishop Fenwick would pay his first visit to Worcester.

It is possible, of course, that sometime in 1826 an itinerant priest made a now-unremembered stopover in Worcester and offered the Mass that was later ascribed to the Jesuit prelate, because practically every stagecoach route in the Northeast traversed Lincoln Square in those days and the U.S. Arms was not only the principal transfer station in the dusty town, but offered accommodations lauded by coachmen and passengers alike. But no records exist to justify such speculation and, given the paucity of priests then serving in New England, it is highly unlikely such a visit would have occurred.

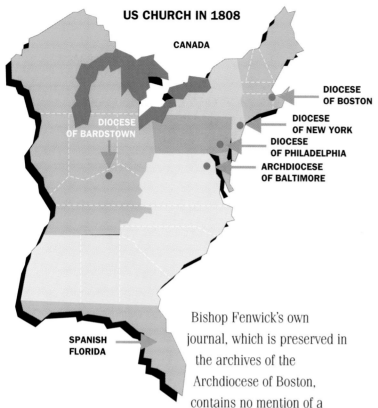

US CHURCH IN 1808

CANADA

DIOCESE
OF BOSTON

DIOCESE
OF NEW YORK

DIOCESE
OF PHILADELPHIA

ARCHDIOCESE
OF BALTIMORE

DIOCESE
OF BARDSTOWN

SPANISH
FLORIDA

Bishop Fenwick's own journal, which is preserved in the archives of the Archdiocese of Boston, contains no mention of a stop in Worcester in 1826 and Robert Johnson-Lally, archivist of the archdiocese, has observed that "judging from the way (the bishop) kept his journal, I find it hard to credit that he would have omitted such an event as saying the first Mass anywhere." It is not until July 27 and Aug. 6, 1832, that journal entries note a visit by the bishop to any central Massachusetts town. On those dates he made overnight stops in Worcester while en route to and from a visit with Father James Fitton, soon to be Worcester County's first resident priest, but who was then in charge of the vast mission in Hartford that included all of Connecticut and stretched into western Massachusetts.

Bishop Fenwick, who was born in 1782 on his father's plantation just outside Leonardtown, Md., was consecrated on Nov. 1, 1825, as Boston's second bishop and was introduced to the congregation in his new cathedral on Dec. 4. He had been ordained a Jesuit priest on June 11, 1808, just two months after Pope Pius VII raised Baltimore to archdiocesan stature and established Boston and New York as two of its four suffragan Sees. At the time, both the newly-restored Society of Jesus and the American Church generally were in such dire need of priests that some of the prerequisites for ordination in the society were waived for him and the others — including his brother, Enoch — who were ordained with him. Benedict spent the first nine years of his priesthood ministering in and around New York City. But in 1817 he was recalled to Maryland and accepted the first of the two appointments he would receive as president of Georgetown College, the nation's oldest Catholic institute of higher learning.

In neither case, however, was Father Fenwick able to complete his presidential term. The first was cut short when he was asked by Baltimore's archbishop to go to South Carolina to try to resolve what had already become known as "the Charleston Schism," and the second ended when he was appointed to succeed Bishop Jean Lefevre de Chevrus, who had returned to France, as bishop of Boston.

When he was sent into the fray in Charleston in late-1818, the confrontation that Catholic University's Father Guilday has recalled as a classic symptom of "America's own peculiar

Bishop Benedict J. Fenwick, S.J.

ecclesiastical disease, 'trusteemania'," had been festering for more than three years. But within a matter of only days, the firm but compassionate Father Fenwick had defused the situation and, in the process, gained invaluable experience. As it turned out, the Charleston upheaval had all the elements that would later disrupt several New England communities during Bishop Fenwick's "watch": ethnic antipathy — in this case Irish parishioners defying the leadership of a French pastor — ambitious and insubordinate priests and lay trustees who claimed all temporal and spiritual authority over their parish, including the right to recruit or remove their pastor.

BUILDING
A PRESBYTERATE FOR NEW ENGLAND

The first challenge Bishop Fenwick faced in his episcopal ministry, however, was far more engrossing — and provides another reason to suspect that he did not visit Worcester in 1826. As a matter of fact, he hardly ever left his See City during that year, so preoccupied was he in trying to recruit and train more priests. The diocese the bishop had been appointed to lead a few months earlier embraced all of New England. Yet, only three priests were available to serve the region and to care for its nine churches — the cathedral in Boston and eight other small gathering places scattered from what Father Robert H. Lord, in his (1944) account of archdiocesan history, termed a "wretchedly dilapidated" Native American chapel in Passamaquoddy, Me., to a "small, unfinished church" in New Bedford.

Even while knowing that there was no surplus of clergy anywhere in the nation, the bishop, nonetheless, presumed to write to several of his brother-bishops and to his Jesuit-friends in Maryland to ask if they would send him or lend him some priests. In the next five years, four exceptional men who had been ministering elsewhere did answer his call and were welcomed into the Boston presbyterate. But Bishop Fenwick's conviction that a local Church should inspire and train its own candidates for the priesthood is, without doubt, what formed the unique personality the Church in New England would retain even to the advent of the 21st Century.

St. Stephen Church, Worcester.

31

Mass is celebrated in the John Henry Cardinal Newman Center at Fitchburg State College, the only free-standing Catholic center on any of the dozen-or-so not-Catholic college or university campuses in Worcester County.

From the moment of his arrival in Boston, Bishop Fenwick ambitioned to build a local seminary. At the outset, of course, few resources were available, so he began simply — by opening his own home to priestly candidates and committing himself as their primary instructor. There is no questioning the success of the endeavor, because in only the next five years nine men who had studied in what came to be known as "the house seminary" were ordained to priesthood — one of whom, Vermont's William Tyler, became the first native New Englander elevated to the hierarchy.

For awhile, in the late-1830s, Bishop Fenwick energetically pursued his dream of making a seminary the centerpiece of the agrarian community he was fostering in Benedicta, Me., the Aroostook County town that, appropriately, was named in his honor. That hope was never realized, but in 1843, the same year that Connecticut and Rhode Island were established as New England's second Catholic diocese and entrusted to the care of Bishop Tyler, the first bishop of Hartford, another agrarian setting — on Mount St. James in Worcester — presented itself and Bishop Fenwick began building an institute that he fancied would both foster

ecclesiastical vocations as well as stimulate intellectual curiosity throughout the diocese. Thus was the College of the Holy Cross born.

When Bishop Fenwick opened his house seminary in April of 1826, the first of the men invited to take up residence was a native Bostonian whose candidacy had been confirmed only a few days after the bishop's arrival from Baltimore — James Fitton. Before death brought an end to nearly 54 years of ministry in 1881, the same James Fitton had earned the reputation that Father Lord, the Boston historian, accorded him later: "the greatest missionary priest in the history of the Diocese of Boston."

Father James Fitton

For all his ministrations, from Boston to the Berkshires, from Bangor to Bridgeport, from Burlington to Bellows Falls to Barnstable, from the byways cut through forests along the Canadian border to the bays and beaches on Long Island Sound, however, no one owes the ubiquitous priest greater homage than do the Catholics of central Massachusetts.

It can be assumed today that Father Fitton did not celebrate the "first Mass" in all the villages where he has been given that credit. And it certainly can be documented that he did not witness Worcester County's first Catholic marriages or perform its first baptisms, as various published accounts have attested over the generations. But then, there is no need to exaggerate either his energy or his accomplishments in order to justify the laurel that is rightly his as the architect of the Holy Roman Apostolic Catholic Church in what, at the dawn of the Third Millennium of Christianity, is the Diocese of Worcester.

Father Fitton not only directed the construction, in Worcester, of the first Catholic church in all of the interior of Massachusetts — alongside a wagon trail that, appropriately, became known as "Temple Street" — but for a decade thereafter used it as a pastoral hub from which he traveled by stagecoach, by chaise and by sleigh, canal boat and railroad handcar, too, to bring the Sacraments and the Mass — in many instances for the first time — to every place in Worcester County where Catholics were then present.

It has been speculated that it was during his visit with Father Fitton in Hartford in early-August of 1832 that Bishop Fenwick asked the young priest to begin including central Massachusetts in his missionary journeys, because as early as

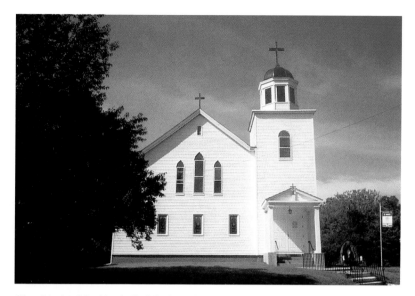

The church of St. Martin Parish, Otter River, the second oldest church in the diocese, was built by Methodists in 1822 and today is the Catholic mother church of northwestern Worcester County, having given birth to 15-plus parishes.

October of that year visits to Webster and Leicester are noted in the marriage register of what was known as the "Hartford Mission." That mission territory, which Father Fitton was serving alone at the time, included the entire State of Connecticut and the four counties of western Massachusetts, yet, by early-1833 he added occasional visits all through the Blackstone River Valley to his itineraries and, in fact, began keeping a sacramental register for what he began calling the "Worcester Mission."

There is no evidence that any priest visited the Massachusetts side of the Blackstone Valley — or anywhere else in Worcester County, for that

St. Michael the Archangel Church, Mendon.

33

matter — during the four years the much-anticipated canal was under construction. But on Oct. 11, 1828, just five days after it was officially opened with the arrival of the "Lady Carrington" at its northern terminus along what later became Worcester Center Boulevard, Father Robert D. Woodley, a priest whom Bishop Fenwick had assigned to Providence early in January of that year, began a two-day visit to Worcester. Presumably, he arrived on another of the canal barges that by then were being drawn regularly to and from Providence. A native Virginian, Robert Woodley had been graduated with distinction from Georgetown in 1825, during the last days of Bishop Fenwick's presidency there, and had recently "made his novitiate in the clerical life," as Boston historians have described it, under Charleston's Bishop John England. He was one of the four men from beyond New England who responded to Bishop Fenwick's earlier plea for priestly help — no doubt with the encouragement of Bishop England who became the first bishop of the southern diocese in 1820, shortly after then-Father Fenwick quelled the "Charleston Schism."

Holy Angels Church in Upton, which lost its roof during the 1938 hurricane and, consequently, also suffered severe interior damage, is one of the 22 former Protestant or Episcopal churches in Worcester County acquired for use by Catholics over the years. Built by Unitarians in 1847, Holy Angels was purchased and renovated for Catholic use in 1869. Today it is one of six former-Protestant churches still being used for worship by Worcester County Catholics, the others being St. Margaret Mary, Our Lady of Fatima and Our Lady of Mercy (Maronite Rite) Churches in Worcester, and St. Denis' in Ashburnham and St. Mary's in Brookfield.

St. Denis Church, East Douglas.

Whether Father Woodley celebrated Mass during his Oct. 11-12, 1828, Worcester visit is undocumented. But Father Robert Lord maintains in Boston's archdiocesan history that since Oct. 12 was a Sunday that year, "in all probability he celebrated the first public Mass" in the town on that day. The primary source of information on the pioneer priest's ministry is his sacramental register and unfortunately, but not surprisingly, it does not include a record of Masses he celebrated. Such registers normally list only ministrations that require written verification such as baptisms performed or marriages witnessed. Precisely documented, however, are 12 baptisms he celebrated that weekend, three on Oct. 11 and nine on the 12th. The first of the ceremonies welcomed into the Church two-month-old Margaret, the daughter of Pierce and Catherine Percy, four-month-old John, the son of Ryan and Mary Murphy, and two-week-old Cornelius, the son of Owen and Catherine Fagan. They are, without question, the first Worcester County baptisms recorded by a Catholic priest and mark the beginning of the sacramental life of Worcester County Catholics.

St. Peter Church, Northbridge.

Father Woodley's sacramental register, which is one of the treasures in the archdiocesan archives in Boston, also details the baptisms of 12 other youngsters during three subsequent Worcester visits on Dec. 28-29, 1828, and on Aug. 31 and Oct. 25, 1829. Since each of those visits also involved a Sunday, Father Lord has speculated that "there can be little doubt" that Father Woodley assembled the town's Catholics for Mass on those occasions, too. But, again, no documentation exists that he did.

Other entries in Father Woodley's sacramental register note visits to South Oxford on May 3, 1829, when he baptized three children and "repeated the marriage ceremony" for three couples; to Dudley and South Oxford on June 28, 1829, when he baptized two two-month-olds; to South Leicester on Aug. 30, 1829, when he baptized a seven-month old boy, and to Uxbridge on Nov. 27, 1829, when he conditionally baptized 33-year-old Mary Mehitable Aldrich before repeating the marriage ceremony uniting her and John Magrath.

Father Woodley was the first priest resident in Rhode Island, but his travels from there to all parts of southern New England rightly led Father Lord to identify him as the first priest of the diocese "who habitually and incessantly traveled over a large area, pursuing every group of Catholics brought to his attention…saying the first Mass in many places…(and) setting an example for the kind of apostolate for which Father Fitton was later to be famous." Unhappily, his New England ministry was short-lived. In late-1830 Father Woodley asked for and received from Bishop Fenwick his release to return to Georgetown and enter the Society of Jesus.

It was in this letter from Father Fitton to Bishop Fenwick, dated Dec. 6, 1833, that the young missionary reports on his "frequent visits to the Catholics of Webster, Dudley, Leicester, Oxford, Millbury and Worcester" and on the "earnest desire (that) has become universal for erecting a church at the last-mentioned town." Written from Hartford and now maintained in the archives of the Archdiocese of Boston, the positive thrust of the letter led to the construction of Christ Church on Temple Street in Worcester, the first Catholic church in the interior of Massachusetts.

A LEGEND
IN THE MAKING

The economic promise of the Blackstone Canal was never realized. One reason, certainly, was that even those who performed the herculean task of designing and building it could not tame the New England winter that left it frozen and unusable for up to four months of the year. Most of all, however, the canal could not compete with the coming of the railroad that by the late-1830s had already begun to dictate the way commerce would be conducted throughout the land.

It is no mere coincidence that the railroad and a second wave of Catholic laborers — many of them recruited directly off the docks in Boston — should make their appearance in central Massachusetts at precisely the same moment that the foundation was being dug for its first Roman Catholic church. This was a pattern that would duplicate itself many times over in the next few decades as railroaders spread their tracks like a spider's web to every compass point in the county.

Dr. Vincent E. Powers, a student of the early-Irish immigration and a professor at Worcester State College, has observed that all the Irish who came to America before the late-1830s were generally literate and, in order to be able to afford the very expensive trans-Atlantic crossing, "had to represent the class of persons who had some money." This may be true, but it is equally true, as a centennial history of St. Mary Parish in Uxbridge observed in 1953, that "most of the railroads in New England (were) built with Yankee dollars and Irish sweat."

When Father Fitton began to make more frequent visits to central Massachusetts in 1833, he centered his ministry in Millbury. The principal reason, no doubt, was because it was two men from that town, John Gaffney and Robert Laverty, who, earlier that year, made the first formal request to Bishop Fenwick for the visitation of a priest. But Millbury was no second-fiddle town, even then. In

Exterior and interior views of St. Patrick Church, Whitinsville.

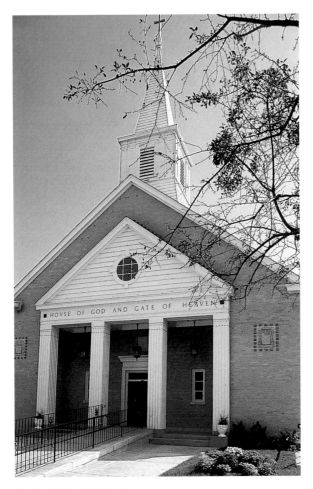

St. Roch Church, Oxford.

St. Anne Church, North Oxford.

fact, while central Massachusetts was still predominantly an agricultural society in the 1830s, Millbury boasted of a vigorous industrial community dating back to the mid-18th Century — a community that even had a powder mill and armory that made weapons for the Continental Army. When it was decided that a Catholic church should be erected to serve the area's growing Catholic population, however, Father Fitton recommended that it be built in the shire town of Worcester, which had been the seat of county government since 1731. In a letter written from Hartford on Dec. 6, 1833, Father Fitton assessed for Bishop Fenwick "the proud prospect for erecting a citadel in the only remaining town of note (without one) on the grand mail-route between Baltimore, Md., and Eastport, Me." Said he:

"By frequent visits to the Catholics of Webster, Dudley, Leicester, Oxford, Millbury and Worcester (all within a circuit of 18 miles),

an earnest desire has become universal for erecting a church at the last-mentioned town, which, while it is the most central, promises to be of much importance. The railway is to commence this end of the route the ensuing spring, which will prove of great assistance towards this desirable object. There are now in Worcester about 20 Catholics; in Millbury, six miles south, there are about the same number; in Leicester, six miles s.w., about the same; in Dudley and the adjacent towns about the same: making in a circuit of about 18 miles, at least one hundred members of the Church, each of whom that I have spoken to on the subject, appears anxious to contribute their mite towards the desired object, severally agreeing that Worcester is the desired site."

Father Fitton gave the bishop "practical proof" of the people's generosity, saying that in addition to pledges they would make toward the building of a church, "they severally promised to pay" from 50 cents to one dollar per month, "provided they had the opportunity of having Mass at least once a month on Sundays. This sum," the missionary told the bishop, "would enable us to buy and pay for a lot of ground by the ensuing spring, when new exertions might be made towards erecting a little church next summer."

The bishop obviously blessed both the proposal and the timetable, because on Sunday, April 6, 1834, the date established by an entry in the diary of Christopher Columbus Baldwin, then the librarian of the American Antiquarian Society, Father Fitton gathered his congregation for an historic Mass in Worcester at which the matter of building a church was probed. While the exact location of that Mass is in dispute, tradition has long held that it was the first one offered by Father Fitton within Worcester's town limits.

*Statue of the Sacred Heart,
Sacred Heart Church, Hopedale.*

The celebrant himself recalled many years later, in an illuminating volume he authored entitled *Sketches of the Establishment of the Church in New England*, that the Mass was held "in the room of a private house, occupied by a worthy mechanic, by name of McKillop, on Front Street, as was the custom over the entire mission, wherever a Catholic family was found to reside." Mr. Baldwin, whose diary reflection placed the gathering "in the new store erected by Mr. Bailey...on the north side of Front Street on the west bank of the Blackstone Canal," said the congregation included worshipers "who came from the factories at Clappville (Leicester) and Millbury" and, using the parlance of the day, numbered "about 60 besides women and children."

Mr. Baldwin, who had received a visit from Father Fitton a few days earlier and may well have been briefed at that time on the priest's

Classic Americana: a mill on "the Blackstone."

Christ Church, Temple Street, Worcester.

ambition to build a Catholic church in the town, wrote in his diary that immediately after the April 6 Mass a total of $600 was pledged by the congregation, $500 "to erect a chapel or church" and $100 to help defray Father Fitton's travel expenses. It was "a princely sum," as Dr. Timothy J. Meagher described it in a sesquicentennial history of St. John Parish in 1984, "in an age when very few men earned as much as half a dollar a day."

Inspired by the generosity of the people, Father Fitton immediately set out to find a plot of land on which to build what would become the mother church of both the Diocese of Springfield and the Diocese of Worcester. And he did find the ideal lot — on the east side of the Worcester Common, at the corner of what were then Salem and Park Streets, near where Notre Dame des Canadiens Church now stands — and purchased it, or so he thought, from a certain "Mr. Browne." When the deed was being drawn in the office of an attorney nearby, however, Mr. Browne

belatedly inquired about the use to which the buyer (dressed in lay clothes as, more often than not, was his custom) intended to put the land.

In his (1899) history of the Springfield diocese, Father John McCoy, long a pastor of St. Anne Parish in Worcester, gives a colorful account of the exchange:

"'What are you to build there?' (Mr. Browne) inquired. 'A Catholic church, sir,' replied Father Fitton. The answer put and end to all negotiations. A coal of fire on the head of the old Puritan could not start him more violently. He hurriedly destroyed the deed and Father Fitton was again obliged to take up the search for land."

That such bigotry should remain from colonial days should not have been overly shocking because, after all, it would be only a matter of a few weeks before what Father Lord has described as "the most disgraceful outrage ever perpetrated in New England and the most tragic event in the history of the Church here" would erupt in Greater Boston.

It was during the night of Aug. 11-12, 1834, that a mob routed 10 defenseless women and 44 terrified children and proceeded to plunder and burn to the ground every building connected with the Ursuline Sisters' convent-school in Charlestown. Not only was Bishop Fenwick's library destroyed, but coffins in the convent

St. John Church, Worcester.

40

mausoleum were opened and the Blessed Sacrament was seized from the tabernacle in the school's chapel and strewn about the grounds or, as was speculated, "carried away as sacrilegious trophies." In subsequent days the ruffians also threatened — with the acquiescence or participation of public officials — to destroy the Cathedral of the Holy Cross. But that threat was never carried out and, in any event, paled in comparison to the atrocity already committed.

It may well be that others in the homogeneous community of Worcester were as horrified as Mr. Browne at the prospect of a Catholic church debasing their predominantly-Congregationalist enclave. Nonetheless, at the same time that agitation against the Ursuline nuns and their students was escalating in Boston three Protestant gentlemen stepped into the breach 44 miles west to mollify the affront Father Fitton had suffered. The canal commissioner, William Lincoln, with the help of Francis Blake and Harvey Pierce, both of whom later entered the Catholic Church, was the principal negotiator in the transaction that was completed on May 1, 1834, making available for Catholic use three lots of pasture land bordering a rutted cart path that ran easterly across what was then known as Flagg's Plain, from Green Street toward the canal. The lots were purchased for $600 and given to Father Fitton. About 18 months would pass before the missionary could repay his benefactors and take formal title to the land, but in the meantime he began regular monthly visits

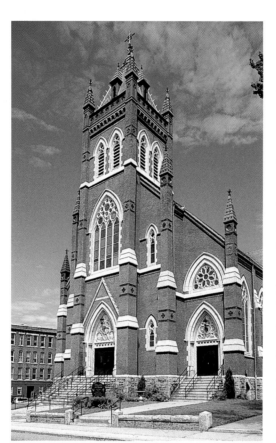

St. John the Evangelist Church, Clinton.

to the town from Hartford and supervised construction of what would be called "Christ Church," the unpretentious structure which, when occupied in 1836, became the mother church of two dioceses and the predecessor of St. John's on Temple Street.

Work on the 32-by-62-feet wood frame structure began almost immediately upon the acceptance of the gift of the land. Early parish notes tell the inspiring story of how, after completing their own long day's work, "Irish railroaders" would gather at the church site each evening to dig the foundation and how, when the digging was sufficient, Father Fitton set, on July 7, 1834, the cornerstone for the building it would support. There was not enough money to complete the entire project that year, but Father Fitton wasted little time in celebrating the first Mass in the completed basement. The faithful are said to have traveled from as far away as Clinton, Westboro and Oxford to join in the joyous celebration with the "four Catholic families, 18 unmarried men and a single lady" whom history records were resident in Worcester at the time. Most early accounts maintain that it was at that Mass in the unroofed basement that nature baptized the congregation when a violent thunderstorm swept across the neighborhood just at the time of the elevation of the Sacred Species. While three men procured umbrellas and held them over the celebrant's head until the storm passed, the people were said to have been "drenched to the skin, but not a single one moved to a place of shelter."

Our Lady of Joy in the courtyard at Chancery, Worcester.

During the next year as the Catholic people watched the completion of their church, Father Fitton oftentimes celebrated Mass on his monthly visits out-of-doors on a "rude altar…amid the wild flowers," as Father McCoy has described the setting, near the "deep cut" between what are now Shrewsbury and Franklin Streets, where the tracks of the Great Western Railroad were quickening the diligent town's imagination. The congregation would have gathered from several towns distant and typically would have included "Irish railroad laborers, Irish maid servants, the stage-drivers, the travelers en route and citizens whom curiosity or other motive brought there." On the Sundays when Father Fitton could not be present, Father McCoy has recalled, "the people went to the church for prayers just as when he was there. Some of the elderly men of the congregation read the prayers of the

Mass and led in the recitation of the litanies," just as they had often done in private homes before they had a priest or a church.

It is interesting to recall a connection to the Church of Worcester that exists, even today, with the extended family of William Lincoln, a noted journalist who, at the time of Father Fitton's arrival in Worcester, was completing work on what would be a highly-acclaimed history of the town.

William was the youngest of the 10 children of Martha Waldo Lincoln and Levi Lincoln (Sr.), an abolitionist attorney who was secretary of state in President Thomas Jefferson's cabinet and who, in 1811, was nominated by President James Madison to fill the first vacancy in the Supreme Court (failing eyesight caused him to decline the honor). Among William's siblings were a brother, Levi (Jr.), who was then completing his ninth one-year term as governor of Massachusetts, and another brother, Enoch, who had recently completed three terms as governor of Maine. It is on the Elm Street property where the younger Levi Lincoln's home was located and where many of the prominent people of the day — including a young congressman from Illinois by the name of Abraham Lincoln — were entertained that the present Chancery Building of the diocese is located.

OPPOSITE PAGE: *Crucifixion window, St. Luke the Evangelist Church, Westboro.*

Chancery Building, Diocese of Worcester.

PERMANENCY
IS ACHIEVED

If the conviction of monks and nuns that no monastery is permanent until the first burial takes place in its cemetery can be extrapolated to a wider population, then the permanency of Catholicism in Worcester County dates not from the completion of Christ Church, but from the burial in what was known as "Tatnuck Cemetery" of John Devanny, a native of County Tipperary in Ireland, who was killed in an accident along the "deep cut" just to the east of Worcester's resurrected Union Station. The cemetery was an acre-and-a-half plot of land on the southerly side of what was then known

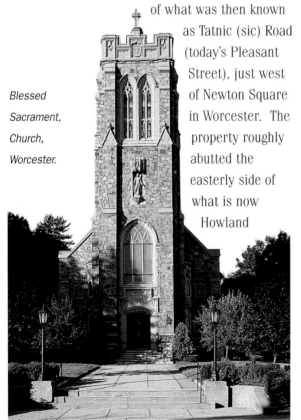

Blessed Sacrament, Church, Worcester.

as Tatnic (sic) Road (today's Pleasant Street), just west of Newton Square in Worcester. The property roughly abutted the easterly side of what is now Howland

Terrace, although that street didn't exist when the land was purchased by Bishop Fenwick for central Massachusetts' first Catholic "burying ground," as the earliest settlers termed it.

Mr. Devanny had been felled — or, more accurately, perhaps, propelled — by a premature blast of "black powder" as the railroad gang of which he was a part was clearing rock in that stretch where the freight yards now run beneath the cliffs of Franklin Street. Witnesses said his body "was hurled a great distance and fell, mangled and torn, in the fork of an adjoining tree." His plight, of course, was repeated throughout central Massachusetts as the railroads made their way west from Boston and on to Springfield and the far reaches of the land, and north to Manchester and Keene and Brattleboro, and south to Providence and New London. The cost in lives and suffering among railroad workers — and before them, among the canal workers — was heavy.

In a monograph he prepared in 1998 for a St. Patrick's Day celebration of the Emerald Club, a county-wide charitable organization, Worcester State's Prof. Vincent Powers put it in numerical perspective:

"It is estimated that at least one Irishman died for every mile constructed for a canal or railway. By 1845 there were over 300 miles of railroads (and nearly 25 miles of canal)

Top of the page: *New England homestead in the north county.*

44

St. Patrick Church and patron, Rutland.

Cemetery. There are even differing accounts as to the number who are reinterred there — and to date there is no central listing of their names.

The location of Tatnuck Cemetery — on what 165 years ago was the outskirts of town — reflected the times. "A more undesirable spot for such a purpose would be difficult to find," is how Richard O'Flynn, a local bookseller and chronicler of the activities of early Worcester-area Catholics, described it in a talk to Worcester's Society of Antiquity in 1897. The land was the only property "that could be obtained," he said, "yet, such as it was the poor pioneers were glad to get it." Those early Catholic settlers, some of whose names Mr. O'Flynn and his son, Thomas, saved for posterity in tracings of headstones in 1876, wanted their own cemetery for obvious sacramental reasons. But they needed it, too, because nativists still refused to allow the bodies of "papists" to contaminate town burial sites.

Mr. Devanny, it should be noted, was not the first Catholic laborer to die hereabouts. That distinction seems to go to one Patrick Joice who was killed in another "black powder" accident, in 1826, as he was unearthing tree stumps in the construction of the Blackstone Canal. But, like others who followed him in death along the banks of the canal and the roadbeds of the region's railroads, his body was shipped to Pawtucket for burial when bigots denied his friends access to a local cemetery plot.

spreading out of Worcester to towns near and far. This represents a great deal of Irish blood."

The accidents had many causes: rush work, untrained workers, inferior materials, explosives. Mr. Devanny, was more fortunate than most, though. He at least had a humane burial. Many other railroaders of the day were simply buried where they fell, giving rise to the popular saying, as Richard Chaisson recalled in a (1988) history of Our Lady Immaculate Parish in Athol: "an Irishman buried under every tie."

Tatnuck Cemetery would tell latter-day Catholics a lot about their roots — about those pioneers who came to Worcester County, mostly from Ireland and French-Canada, in the early decades of the 19th Century. Unfortunately, little about who was buried there has yet been documented. Indeed, those who were buried there have rested anonymously and ignored in recent generations in a mass grave excavated for their remains across Middle River in St. John

St. John Cemetery, Worcester. "Giants," all!

45

Bishop Fenwick purchased the Tatnic Road site from Rejoice Newton on Aug. 6, 1835, exactly 33 days after the first railroad train arrived in Worcester from Boston (July 4, 1835). It became the principal place of burial for the Catholics of the county for about a dozen years. But by 1848, the same year that Worcester became a city, the ecumenical climate had improved enough so that Bishop John B. Fitzpatrick, the brother-in-law of the noted Worcester contractor, Tobias Boland, and Bishop Fenwick's successor in Boston, was able to purchase from the legendary Eli Thayer, the first eight-plus acres of land for another cemetery — just off the road between the center of the infant city and what by then was known as Holy Cross College. Entrusted to the care of the mother parish, over time St. John Cemetery would be the largest of the 40 Catholic cemeteries that would be developed in Worcester County.

For all practical purposes "Tatnuck Cemetery" was closed when that first land for St. John's was obtained, but burials appear to have continued for some years thereafter, primarily, it is believed, for family members of persons already interred there. After a request to purchase the property for residential development was made to Bishop Thomas D. Beaven, the second bishop of Springfield, the Massachusetts Legislature, in an act dated March 7, 1903, authorized the closure of the cemetery.

The legislators granted the bishop permission to remove the decedents and directed that he "select and provide suitable places for the re-interments," that "all monuments and headstones shall be

The burial site of Msgr. Thomas F. Griffin, long-time chancellor of the Diocese of Springfield and pastor of St. John Parish, at St. John Cemetery, Worcester.

carefully removed and re-set when others are not provided" and that "the places of second burial shall be indicated upon a suitable plan of the cemetery or cemeteries" designated by the bishop. According to records in St. John Cemetery, in June of 1907 Murray Brothers, undertakers, removed 2,005 bodies from the west side site and reinterred them at St. John's. Records at the board of health are not consistent in every respect with those at St. John's, but five of the decedents exhumed in Tatnuck — all military veterans — are believed to have been reinterred in the so-called "Soldier's Plot" in the new cemetery while the remaining 2,000 were placed in the mass grave across Middle River, along the line where St. John's property abuts that of Hope Cemetery — their banishment to the far reaches of obscurity being repeated, but this time by "their own kind."

A (1931) book entitled *Old Landmarks and Historic Spots of Worcester, Massachusetts* observed that "the poet who wrote the poem describing an early New England graveyard must have heard of the Tatnuck Cemetery" (possibly, too, the barren, chill, dispiriting plot to which it was removed):

"'The dreariest part of all the land,
To death they set apart,

A horticultural request from the decedents in Mary, Queen of the Rosary Cemetery, Spencer.

46

Memorial to deceased members of the Ninth Infantry Division, U.S. Army, overlooking Gold Star Boulevard, at Immaculate Conception Church, Worcester.

With scanty grace from Nature's hand
And none at all from Art'."

With the Church's permanency established in a growing central Massachusetts and with more priests becoming available to visit the far reaches of New England, sometime in late-1835 Bishop Fenwick asked Father Fitton about moving his residence from Hartford to Worcester. His reply, contained in a letter from the Connecticut city dated Jan. 26, 1836, and reserved in the archdiocesan archives, appears ambiguous. The priest said it was "evident...that I can be of greater service to the interests of religion in Worcester than in this city," but he adds:

"Worcester, alone, yet in its infancy, and having a church to build, cannot be expected to provide for the maintenance of a clergyman immediately. I wish to see the church firmly established, a school in being and whatever debt thereby contracted — liquidated — which I promise to do by attending the Norwich Railroad which will go on in the spring."

Apparently progress was swifter than expected because only four months later, on an unknown day in May of 1836, Father Fitton became the first priest to take up permanent residence in central or western Massachusetts and by the end of that year had liquidated the debt on Christ Church. He then established not one, but two schools, one, for religious education, in the basement of the church and the other on a 52-acre prominence he had purchased about two miles south of Temple Street. Although any boy in the parish who had reached his eighth birthday could apply for admission to the school on what Native Americans had called the "Hill of Pleasant Springs," Father Fitton's intent was to open a boarding school there for "the advanced education of Catholic young men." Eventually he built a two-story school building and dormitory on the site, along with a small frame

O'Kane Hall at the College of the Holy Cross, Worcester.

Prince of Peace Church, Princeton

cottage that became his parish residence. There, too, as Dr. Meagher put it in St. John's sesquicentennial history, "students and faculty alternated their studies with work on the wheat fields and grape vineyards of the surrounding farm land and simultaneously laid the foundation for New England's first Catholic college, Holy Cross."

Father Fitton, who was born in Boston on April 10, 1805, and was baptized by the illustrious Father Matignon, confirmed by the saintly Bishop Chevrus and ordained, on Dec. 23, 1827, by the indefatigable Bishop Fenwick, must have felt right at home at the farm on what he christened "Mount St. James," in honor of his baptismal patron. On most days as a youngster on his way to school, after all, James would drive his father's cows to pasture on Boston Common and return at each day's end to gather them home again.

While the missionary's new "parish" initially extended far beyond the confines of Worcester County, it was here that he spent most of his energy, taking particular note of the shanty towns along the route of the Great Western Railroad and the mill villages all through the Blackstone Valley. His ministrations in Auburn, Grafton, Westboro, Millbury, Northbridge, Uxbridge, Sutton, Blackstone, Oxford, Charlton, Webster, Dudley, Leicester, Spencer, the Brookfields, Barre, Warren and Templeton are well documented. There were no churches, but reverence was as deep in the private homes or

Windows, St. Joseph Church, Charlton.

48

local schoolhouses or taverns (with hanging quilts or blankets hiding the bottles from view) when he set up his altar. Oftentimes, too, a gandy dancer would take him by handcar along the railroad bed to offer Mass in a laborer's shanty or, in good weather, out-of-doors in a grove of evergreens or in the gentle embrace of a sheltering oak or maple or chestnut tree.

It was Masses at the mother church on Temple Street, however, that most represented the universality of the Church. The altar was regularly prepared by Mary Davis, a Black woman who had followed Father Fitton from Hartford, and the congregation invariably included not only richer and poorer Irish-Catholics who might have walked or arrived by carriage from towns near and far, but English converts and travelers passing through town, as well as curious Protestants. And, as French-Canadians began to take up residence in the region, they, too, became part of the congregation as, for a few weeks every summer, did Penobscot Indians from Maine, among whom Father Fitton had ministered during the first year of his priesthood. During his years at Christ Church, the Native Americans — men, women and children — made an annual month-long pilgrimage to visit with their old friend and upon arriving would pitch their tents "at the foot of Temple Street." In a 1910 article in *Worcester Magazine,* Father John McCoy painted a pensive word-picture:

"(The Penobscots) came every Sunday to the Mass in solemn procession and assisted with every sign of respect and adoration. After Mass, they had a custom of gathering in a circle outside the church door and there, kneeling on the ground, awaited the coming of the priest. After his thanksgiving (after Mass), Father Fitton, who knew their habits, went out into the circle, lightly laying his hand on each bowed head in benediction. They then rose, satisfied, and went their way."

FATHER FITTON'S
ENDURING GIFT

Father Fitton's academy progressed well during its formative years. It was attracting students from Maine to Texas. But he realized that his responsibilities to isolated Catholics at far-flung Mass stations were his priority. Therefore, in order to assure its future prosperity, as well as to aid his mentor in realizing a dream of a seminary for New England, the stalwart priest turned the fortunes of his cherished school over to Bishop Fenwick on Feb.

Worcester as seen from "a beautiful eminence" overlooking the town.

2, 1843 — only a few months, as it turned out, before he would accept an assignment to Providence. The bishop immediately invited Jesuits at Georgetown, in the nation's capital, to staff the institute which was located, as he wrote to them, "on a beautiful eminence (commanding) the view of the whole town of Worcester," and began construction of a new dormitory and classroom building. The day the cornerstone for that brick structure was set, June

Burial site of Father Joseph T. O'Callahan, S.J., in the Jesuit Cemetery at Holy Cross College. A war-time Navy chaplain, he was awarded the Congressional Medal of Honor for heroic service in the South Pacific aboard the fabled U.S.S. Franklin.

21, 1843, was one of the most triumphal in the early history of Catholicism in central Massachusetts. A grand procession, with bands and banners, escorted the bishop and his party from the railroad station downtown to the campus where New York's Father C. Constantine Pise, acclaimed at the time as the nation's most eloquent Catholic orator, delivered an address intended as much to assuage the fears of the wider community as to inspire the teachers and students who would soon be interacting there. Some sources claim that President John Tyler, who had taken part in the dedication of Boston's Bunker Hill Monument four days earlier, had been invited to take part in the ceremonies on Mount St. James, but a death within his cabinet prevented it. Among those who were present, however, was New York's Father John

McCloskey who, 33 years later, while serving as the archbishop of New York, would become the United States' first cardinal.

In his talk at the dedication — an address reprinted in its entirety by Father Fitton in his *Sketches* — Father Pise acknowledged the "misgivings" and "misapprehensions" the general community might be harboring over the founding of New England's first Catholic college — and a "Jesuit one" at that! But he reassured his listeners that:

"The youth who will here be formed to letters will also be molded into true Christians and sincere republicans. They will be taught first the necessity of religion, the practice of virtue, the maxims of charity; afterwards, an entire devotion to the glorious institutions of our country. They will be instructed to recognize no temporal power over this free land in any foreign authority, whether secular or ecclesiastic. They will be taught that even the sovereign Pontiff, whose spiritual jurisdiction, as Catholics, we admit and revere, possesses and claims no right to exercise any sway over

Notre Dame des Canadiens Church, Worcester.

us as citizens of this great republic....They will be taught, within these walls, to give to God the things that are God's, and to Caesar the things that are Caesar's. And the eternal truth of this maxim will be deeply inculcated: that he who is not faithful to his country, will not be true to his God."

Father Pise's prophecy may never have been better illustrated than on an obscure island in the South Pacific Ocean one day shy of 99 years after Bishop Fenwick took title to Father Fitton's Academy when the gallantry of Lt. John V. Power, a Holy Cross alumnus who grew up in Worcester's St. Paul Parish, caused a grateful nation to award him the Congressional Medal of Honor, posthumously. It was on Feb. 1, 1944, that the young Marine officer, who was later memorialized with an heroic-size statue on the

Statue at Worcester's City Hall of Marine Lt. John V. Power, Congressional Medal of Honor winner in World War II, who grew up in St. Paul Parish.

Franklin Street side of Worcester's City Hall, gave his life while storming a fortified enemy gun emplacement on Namur Island, Kwajalein Atoll, in the Marshall Islands as American forces relentlessly made their way toward the Japanese home islands during World War II. Mystically, the senior thesis he had written three years earlier in completion of the requirements for his Holy Cross diploma was a study of "The Ethics of War."

Apparently, however, the Legislature's so-

called "Nunnery Committee," whose task it was to assure that "nothing seditious or rebellious or unpatriotic" was going on in any Catholic institution in the commonwealth, was not overly impressed by Father Pise's assertions at the dedication because 22 years would pass before nativist lawmakers would authorize Holy Cross to grant academic degrees in its own name. In the meantime, the faculty and trustees of Georgetown, whence most of the Holy Cross instructors had come, rewarded the Worcester scholars.

There was a large void when the first 12 Holy Cross students began classes on Nov. 1, 1843. An obedient Father Fitton was absent from the town. Just as Bishop Fenwick's first appointment as a college president was abbreviated by the menace of trusteeism in South Carolina, so was Father Fitton's tenure in Worcester County brought to an end when that dreaded ache reared its ugly head in Rhode Island. Bishop Fenwick, by that time, had attracted or ordained more than 30 priests to minister with him in the six-state region but, apparently, he felt the one best suited to heal a rift that had engulfed what would later become Providence's Cathedral of SS. Peter and Paul was his own first ordinand.

Interior and exterior views of Ascension Church, Worcester.

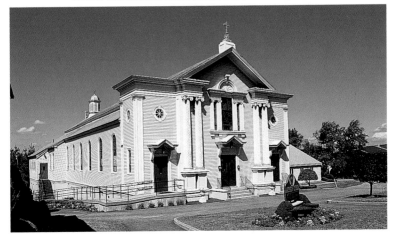

St. John the Baptist Church, East Brookfield.

Revered at the time of his death as the "patriarch" of New England priests, Father Fitton was buried in Holy Cross Cemetery in Malden following the arrival there of what Father Lawrence P. McCarthy, his successor at Holy Redeemer, later described in a tribute to him as "the largest funeral cortege, by far, that ever left East Boston."

Father Adolphus Williamson, who had come from Baltimore to help Bishop Fenwick, was assigned to succeed Father Fitton as Worcester County's priest-in-residence. Unfortunately, sickness necessitated his return to the South after only 18 months and, on April 6, 1845, Father Matthew W. Gibson, an emigrant from England, was appointed to pastor Christ Church, a congregation that by then numbered some 2,000 souls and served 12 "outmissions." Despite any shortcomings in his own personality, Father Gibson initiated a period of phenomenal growth for the Church in the region. Before he would leave in January of 1856 for Wisonsin and then back to his native England, he would have built nine churches and laid the foundations for a dozen Worcester County parishes.

The turmoil began in the Providence parish after the bishop transferred its popular pastor and, despite a personal appeal from a "committee of seven parishioners," refused to reinstate him. In protest, the committee seized all the temporalities of the parish, including the keys to the church and to the tabernacle. Father Fitton was obviously well-taught at the house seminary because just as his mentor had promptly defused the stand-off in Charleston, so did he, on only his second day in Providence, restore peace to the turbulent parish there.

Father Fitton remained in the Rhode Island capital for about a year, but after his friend, Father William Tyler, was consecrated as bishop of Hartford and took up residence in Providence, where the majority of Catholics in the new two-state diocese resided, the eminent missionary moved on to Newport. He served there until returning to Boston where, for the 26 years prior to his death on Sept. 15, 1881, he was pastor of Most Holy Redeemer Parish.

From the very outset, however, Father Gibson sparked negative reactions among his people. Describing him in the (1984) sesquicentennial history of St. John's as

St. Bernard Church, Worcester.

"aristocratic and overbearing," Dr. Meagher said Father Gibson's appointment to Worcester was "a little like touching a match to a powder keg." Where Father Fitton often wore "simple workingmen's clothes," Dr. Meagher wrote, "the haughty Gibson insisted on wearing clerical garb as well as a fancy overcoat adorned with a luxuriant purple and white collar." But the greater affront was in putting down traditions that had already taken hold within the Worcester congregation. While Father Fitton, by reason of temperament, had encouraged the involvement of the laity in parish affairs and Father Williamson, for reasons of his health, had welcomed it, Father's Gibson's style was to assert clerical authority at every turn.

Nonetheless, the people heartily supported their new pastor's pursuit of Father Fitton's dream of building a new, larger, more permanent church on the site of the old. Christ Church, which would be renamed "The Institute" and would serve the parish as a social/educational

St. Margaret Mary Church, Worcester.

center for another 90 years, was moved to an adjacent lot, and within a little more than a year the new brick church, topped by an inspiring steeple that rose 136 feet into the Worcester skyline, was completed on the original site. Described as a "fine example" of Greek Revival church architecture, the building was blessed by then-Coadjutor Bishop John B. Fitzpatrick of Boston on June 24, 1846, in the presence of an ailing Bishop Fenwick, Father Fitton, some 30 other priests and a standing room-only congregation. While steeple renovations carried out in conjunction with the parish's 150th anniversary celebration in 1984 hinted that Bishop Fitzpatrick may have placed the church under the dual patronage of "Our Lady and St. John," tradition has held that it was named after the baptismal patron of the officiating bishop, St. John the Evangelist. Interestingly, however, Bishop Fitzpatrick chose as the date for the dedication, the Feast of the Nativity of St. John the Baptist.

The zealous Bishop Fenwick, who was suffering from heart disease, would survive only seven weeks beyond the dedication of St. John's. On Aug. 11, 1846 — by strange coincidence, 12 years to the day after the assault on his cherished convent-school in Charlestown — he

The sanctuary of Our Lady of Mount Carmel Church, Worcester.

Our Lady of the Rosary Church, Worcester.

died, peacefully, at his home near the Boston cathedral. Two days later, following a Funeral Mass celebrated by Bishop Fitzpatrick and a triumphal procession of thousands through the streets of Boston to the railroad terminal, an estimated 1,000 mourners boarded a train for the trip to Worcester where another procession formed and escorted the funeral carriage to "the grave chosen and indicated by himself" in the Jesuit cemetery at Holy Cross College where he rests today. A *Golden Jubilee Souvenir* history of the present St. John Church, published in 1896 on the 50th anniversary of its dedication, maintains that "a few days before his death (Bishop Fenwick) ceded to the Society (of Jesus) full control and possession of the institution which he had founded. The buildings and grounds were transferred to the Fathers and the only

return asked was the provision for the diocese, of one free scholarship for every 50 students."

Immediately upon Bishop Fenwick's death he was succeeded by Bishop Fitzpatrick who served the Church all across Massachusetts until the elevation of Bishop John J. Williams in 1866, four years before the then-five county Diocese of Springfield was established and nine years before Boston was raised to the dignity of an archdiocese.

As Boston's Father Lord has written, Bishop Fenwick's episcopate, "in the face of the gravest difficulties...marked the great turning point in the fortunes of the Church in New England." Without doubt, he observed, "if Father Matignon and Bishop Chevrus are the true founders of the Diocese of Boston, Bishop Fenwick deserves to be called its organizer."

Similarly it can be said that if Father Fitton was the architect of the Church in central Massachusetts, so Father Gibson was its first contractor.

Interior of Holy Name of Jesus Church, Worcester.

Our Lady of Fatima Church, Worcester.

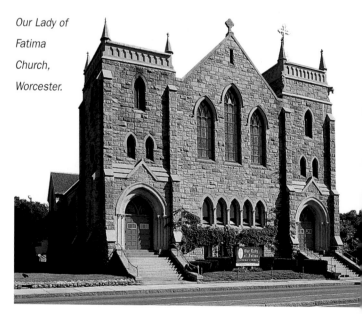

RAPID GROWTH
BECOMES A REALITY

In the years immediately following the opening of St. John Church, Father Gibson, assisted by the Jesuits at Holy Cross and the other priests who eventually came to reside at the mother church, not only established the Church firmly in the mill villages that continued to thrive along the Blackstone River — even after the quixotic canal era ended in 1848 — but in the hamlets in northern Worcester County that grew from the shanty towns to which the railroads gave birth. During the decade he ministered hereabouts, Father Gibson supervised the construction of seven churches — St. Anne's in Worcester; St. Polycarp's, the precursor of all other churches in Leicester; St. Bernard's in Fitchburg; St. Luke's, the first of five churches in four locations with three names in West Boylston; St. Louis' in Webster; St. Bridget's (sic) in Millbury and St. Martin's in the Otter River section of Templeton. In addition he arranged the purchase of two former Baptist churches and renovated them for Catholic use by congregations dedicated to St. Leo in Leominster and to St. Catherine of Siena

in Athol. He also organized congregations in Grafton, Milford, Uxbridge Northbridge, Southbridge, Spencer, Holden, Clinton, Gardner, Barre and Winchendon.

There is little question that the oldest priest ever to have served in Worcester County was also the first "curate" assigned to the area. Well, whether he was actually assigned for active ministry or as a companion for Father Gibson must be questioned, because when Father T. A. McAvoy arrived at St. John's in 1846, just after the new church was blessed, he was, roughly, 83 years of age. Little biographical information is available concerning him, unfortunately, but, according to Father Cornelius M. Foley, who built the present St. Bernard Church in Fitchburg in 1869 and who was with Father McAvoy when he died in 1874, the elder priest was "in his 111th year" when he breathed his last. Father McAvoy (the diocesan necrology for Springfield lists only a Father James A. McEvoy among priest-deaths in 1874) had remained with Father Gibson in Worcester for only about a year, it appears, before moving to Fitchburg where Father Gibson had established a second home and where he stayed while ministering in that part of his extensive "parish." In his history of the Springfield diocese Father McCoy recalls that Father McAvoy whose "mind was clear," even at the

TOP OF THE PAGE: *Icon of the Nativity in Our Lady of Perpetual Help (Melkite Rite) Parish, Worcester*

Our Lady of Good Counsel Church, West Boylston, the fifth church in the fourth location with the third name serving those neighborhoods.

end, "said Mass regularly until within five years of his death." Father McCoy also observed that while Father McAvoy was not able to do much work in his later years, "his presence made it possible for Father Gibson to give more of his time and service to the missions."

The histories of the emerging Catholic congregations continued to be wonderfully entwined with the history of the mother church until the new mission centers evolved in Millbury and Milford and Webster and Clinton and Fitchburg and Otter River to serve the new waves of poor immigrants. As Father Richard D. McGrail, a modern-day Worcester diocesan historian, wrote in 1990:

Windows in St. Casimir Church, Worcester.

"Smitten by life-destroying famine and government folly, the Irish came. Pawns on the chessboard of conflicting governments, the

Italians came. Tossed about by economic depression and accompanying unemployment, the French-Canadians came. Downtrodden by foreign tyrants and alien arms, the Polish came, and the Lithuanians."

Later, whether driven by economic or political oppression at home or merely by a thirst to taste America's promise, the Portuguese came, and Slovaks came from central Europe and Syrians and Lebanese also came. Later still, came Cubans and Ecuadorians and Brazilians and others from a score of Latin American nations. And Vietnamese and Cambodians and Laotians and others from all across southeast Asia also came. Together they, and African-Americans who migrated from other sections of the nation, became the heart and soul, the body and blood of the Church of Worcester where, even as the 21st Century was dawning, Mass was being celebrated regularly in a dozen languages.

Simultaneously with the arrival in central Massachusetts in the 1840s and 1850s of refugees from the Irish famine, French-Canadians began to arrive in growing numbers. Members of Notre Dame des Canadiens Parish in Worcester and Notre Dame Parish in Southbridge, both established in 1869, have long debated which of them is the mother parish of the more than a score of "French-Canadian Parishes" established in Worcester County over the years. However, if the documents used in compiling the 1944 history of the Boston archdiocese are to be believed, the history of the first French-language parish in Worcester County is also the history of the first French-language parish in all of New England and it culminates in 1856 with the founding of St. Anne Parish on what today is known as Shrewsbury Street.

Interior of Our Lady of Czestochowa Church, Worcester.

56

The influence of more recent immigrants to Worcester County is shown in the bi-lingual sign identifying St. Peter Church, Worcester, and in the statue of St. Andrew Dung Lac Tran, a 19th-Century Vietnamese martyr, in the yard at St. John Church, Worcester.

That story began on Oct. 23, 1846, when Father Zéphyrin Lévesque, a newly-arrived priest of the Quebec diocese, was sent by Bishop Fitzpatrick to visit Worcester and the neighboring towns where French-Canadians were known to be living, to determine just how many of his countrymen were actually there. After reporting that he found about 150 families, the bishop placed them under the priest's care — along with "the Canadian Catholics of Manchester, N.H., among those of other places," thereby establishing, Boston historians maintain, "the first French-Canadian parish of the diocese under Bishop Fitzpatrick." Father Lévesque took up residence at St. John's, but soon found that his people were uncomfortable worshiping in the Temple Street church, not only for cultural reasons, but because the Irish members of the community were in direct competition with them for jobs. And, of course, since the end of the French and Indian War in 1763 the Canadians had

associated the language spoken at St. John's — English — with English suppression in Canada.

Father Lévesque attempted to establish what today might be called a French-Canadian mission, or at least a Mass "station," on a third floor hall on Main Street, but as Richard L. Gagnon records in *A Parish Grows Around the Common*, his (1995) history of Notre Dame des Canadiens Parish, "after six months he fell ill and had to go to New Orleans to recuperate." Before Father Lévesque left, however, he turned over to Bishop Fitzpatrick the $200 already collected for a proposed French-language church — a sum said to have been returned

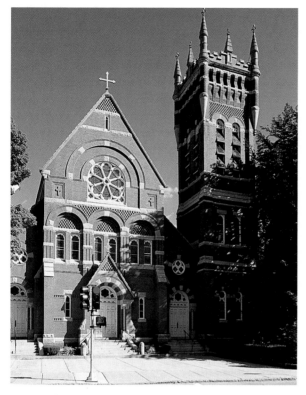

St. Peter Church, Worcester.

to him when he was named pastor of the new St. Bridget Parish in Millbury on Oct. 1, 1851, the day before that church was blessed by the bishop.

After Father Lévesque's departure for Louisiana, the care of the French-Canadian Catholics fell again to Father Gibson and to Irish-born Father John Boyce, a novelist who gained literary fame writing under the nom de plume "Paul Peppergrass" and who was appointed in 1847 to serve with Father Gibson as co-pastor of St. John's. The two men did accomplish much together, but not always in harmony. Father Boyce's eloquence in the pulpit and his caring and concern out of it immediately helped to reestablish bonds of trust between the priests and people of the town. But one of the things that divided the two men was the care of the French-speaking members of the congregation. With the entire Catholic population in the area increasing, Father Boyce believed the seating capacity at St. John's should be expanded to accommodate everyone, while Father Gibson sympathized with the French-Canadians' desire for a church of their own. As it turned out, since they had equal authority as co-pastors, each man followed his own plan: Father Boyce increased the size of the Temple Street structure and Father Gibson became involved in the formation of a new congregation — St. Anne's on today's Shrewsbury Street.

Father Matthew Gibson

Father John Boyce

OPPOSITE PAGE: *The Ascension mural in St. Francis of Assisi Church, Athol.*

SIMPLE CROSSES
AND ELABORATE WEATHER VANES

While several other parishes had been formed in the Blackstone Valley before St. Bernard's in Fitchburg was established in early-1856, it was in that north county town that Catholic settlers erected the first church outside of Worcester topped by a simple cross rather than an elaborate weather vane.

St. Bernard Church, Fitchburg.

When the first Mass was celebrated in Fitchburg, and by whom, is uncertain, although Father Gibson began visiting there irregularly soon after the rail line from Boston was completed on March 5, 1845. At that time, it is said, there were only two permanent Catholic residents in town. Within two years, however, when the Catholic population had swelled to 500, the Worcester-based priest not only announced he would begin visiting them on the second Sunday of each month but began formulating plans to build a small church that would be St. John's first formal mission. He accomplished the feat and on March 12, 1848, celebrated the first Mass in the 20-by-30-feet chapel that was appropriately dubbed "the shanty cathedral" because it was built with wood salvaged from the shanties "the railroaders" had lived in as they set the ties and laid the tracks that first linked all the towns of northern Worcester County to the universe.

St. Philip Benizi Church, Grafton.

Top of the page: *a sketch of "the shanty cathedral" in Fitchburg, the first mission church of St. John's in Worcester.*

St. James Church, South Grafton

It is unclear whether a 25-by-40-feet chapel in Grafton that was subsequently dubbed "the church with gypsy blood" because it was moved to the Cherry Valley section of Leicester and reconstructed as "St. Polycarpe's" and then moved to the Rochdale section of Leicester and reconstructed as "St. Aloysius'" predated "the shanty cathedral." But, if it did — and it is questioned whether such a structure was under the patronage of St. Mark or St. Philip — the missionaries from Worcester long considered Grafton a Mass "station" and not a "mission," in the sense that Fitchburg became.

Whatever the case, prosperity accompanied the railroad to Fitchburg and the Catholic population mushroomed to the point that even before 1848 was over Father Gibson was marshaling members of the community to dig the foundation for a larger, more permanent church there. He intended that it be built "of granite," but because of what, without

St. Mary Church, North Grafton.

great elaboration, was termed, "disunity" within the congregation, money ran out and the basement had to be roofed over. It remained a "basement church," then, until March 6, 1852, when a violent wind — that, as it turned out, was a blessing in disguise — blew the roof away.

Happily, in adversity the community healed its wounds and rather than simply replacing the roof on the foundation, it constructed a wood frame superstructure over it that Bishop Fitzpatrick dedicated to St. Bernard — his secondary baptismal patron — on Sept. 18, 1852. That church remained the gathering place for the parish established in January, 1856, with Father Edward Turpin as pastor, until Mass was celebrated for the first time, on Christmas Day, 1869, in the much larger and "more permanent" brick church where parishioners of the mother church of the north county still worship.

The first parish in Worcester County carved from territory entrusted to the priests of St. John's, was centered in Milford where, on Feb. 4, 1850, three months after Bishop Fitzpatrick had dedicated a new church to St. Mary of the Assumption, Father George A. Hamilton, recently pastor in St. Albans, Vt., was appointed to lead what came to be known

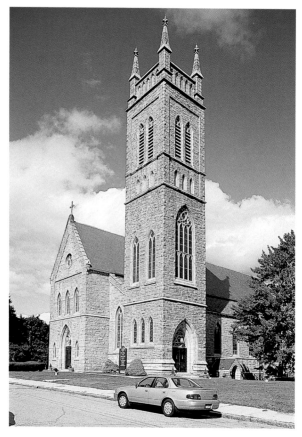

St. Mary of the Assumption Church, Milford.

as "The Great Milford Parish." It could not compare in size, of course, to the geographic area that Father Fitton and Father Gibson had tended. Still, Father Hamilton had the care of missions in Framingham and Hopkinton and so-called Mass "stations" in Southboro, Holliston, Upton, Westboro and Marlboro, and was expected to celebrate Mass and the Sacraments as often as possible in Maynard, Medway, Natick, Stow, Sudbury, Needham, Ashland, Weston and Wayland.

The first Masses in Milford were probably celebrated by Father Fitton in private homes "before 1843," but when the Catholic population began to grow, Father Gibson sought and received authorization to use the Town Hall as a gathering place for worship. As happened later in several other places, however, Protestant frenzy caused an almost immediate withdrawal of the permission until, as Father McCoy put it in his history of the Springfield diocese, "some of the more liberal Protestants protested…against the unfairness (and) succeeded in shaming the bigots."

By the time the roadbed of the Providence railroad had reached Milford from Framingham in 1848, the Catholic community had outgrown the Town Hall facilities and Father Boyce gathered his congregation together to discuss building a church of their own. The wood frame structure that was subsequently completed and dedicated to Our Lady by Bishop Fitzpatrick on Nov. 4, 1849, served the parish for 20 years. Then, on Christmas Day, 1869 — at the same time the first Masses were being celebrated in the new Church of St. Bernard in Fitchburg, the mother parish of the north county — the first Masses were also celebrated in the new church of the mother parish of the south county, St. Mary of the Assumption, Milford. That church in Milford, which still serves that parish, was built under the guidance of Father Patrick Cuddihy, a native of Ireland and friend of the famed Irish rebel, Daniel O'Connell, who, before construction began, purchased a quarry in town containing the pink granite used in the construction of all the parish buildings.

While energetic and resourceful, Father Cuddihy was not universally beloved. Indeed, Father Michael G. Foley, pastor of St. Mary's when the parish was celebrating its 150th anniversary, said "the word that best described Father Cuddihy was 'curmudgeon'." He then related a story told to him by an elderly parishioner whose father had been a long-time

Sacred Heart of Jesus Church, Milford.

St. Paul the Apostle Church, Blackstone.

custodian in the parish. "The custodian claimed," Father Foley said, "that when Father Cuddihy was being buried at the base of the Irish round tower he built in the parish cemetery — also with pink granite — the ropes the pall bearers were using to lower the casket into the grave slipped and there was a loud banging as the casket hit the tower's foundation stones. Said the young curate attending the pastor, 'My lord, can't you even go to your grave without making a fuss?'"

At the time of his death in late-1898, just before his 90th birthday, Father Cuddihy had been pastor in Milford for more than 40 years and was not only the oldest priest in the United States, but the oldest in years of priestly service, having been ordained in Rome in 1831, almost 67 years to the day earlier.

The next parish formed — the third in the present Diocese of Worcester — was established in Blackstone on Nov. 23, 1850, and was dedicated to St. Paul the Apostle. The original parish church, built not too far from the railroad tracks that became the lifeblood of the mills and factories that enticed and sustained an ever-increasing number of immigrant workers and

their families, is still in use, although greatly enlarged. It was built on land donated by Welcome Farnum, a member of St. John (Episcopal) Church who had not only brought skilled Irish wool weavers from Ireland to work in his mills but later offered employment to many skilled and unskilled canal and railroad workers. It is said that Mr. Farnum, whose brother-in-law was Worcester-born George Bancroft, who founded the United States Naval Academy at Annapolis while serving as President James K. Polk's secretary of the Navy and who authored the first (10-volume) history of the United States, also encouraged his Catholic workers to take time from their mill jobs — without any loss of wages — to help complete their house of worship. The structure was built with granite quarried nearby and is not only the second oldest church built by Catholics in the Diocese of Worcester, but may well be the only church in the United States that straddles a state line, its sanctuary and aula being in Blackstone and a portion of its façade and entryway rising from the soil of Smithfield, R.I.

While Father Woodley may have visited the town from Woonsocket, R.I., as early as 1828, it is widely accepted that in 1834 Father Fitton celebrated Mass for many of the 30 Catholics then living there, in "the home of Edward McCabe." Blackstone was one of the few towns that didn't lose contact with Father Fitton after he left Worcester for Rhode Island, because he regularly visited Woonsocket where there was a large Catholic settlement. But it remained for Father Charles O'Reilly, a kinsmen of Bishop Bernard O'Reilly, the second bishop of Hartford, to build St. Charles Church in Woonsocket, with the help of people from Blackstone, and to build

St. Paul's in Blackstone, with the help of people from Woonsocket. In fact, as construction on the Blackstone building was beginning in late-1850, Father O'Reilly, a native of Ireland who had been a missionary in the West Indies before journeying to New England, requested a transfer from the Hartford diocese to the Boston diocese. Whether he liked Blackstone better than Woonsocket is uncertain. What is certain is that a bitter feud had developed between himself and his cousin, the bishop. When he left Woonsocket for his new assignment, Father O'Reilly brought with him the deeds to property he had purchased for a cemetery for St. Charles Parish, land that became the cemetery of the Blackstone parish. Bishop Fitzpatrick dedicated the parish church to St. Paul on July 11, 1852.

During the next three years, as the Catholic population in "the valley" burgeoned, Father Gibson organized the building of St. Bridget Church in Millbury and St. Louis' in Webster, while Father O'Reilly, who had come to know the people of Uxbridge while in Woonsocket as well as Blackstone, laid the foundation for the first St. Mary Church there. It is known that Father Woodley visited Uxbridge in 1829 and while he undoubtedly celebrated Mass on that occasion, the "first Mass of record" in the town was celebrated in the late-winter

or early-spring of 1850 by Father Patrick McGrath who had joined Father Hamilton in ministry at the Milford parish. Thereafter Mass was celebrated irregularly in private homes, but when a priest could not be there on Sunday they, like Catholics throughout the area at the time, most often went to where the priest would be. As the (1953) centennial history of the Uxbridge parish said:

> "Few, if any, could afford to ride, but they could walk and they did walk, shank's mare, over the rough roads powdered with dust in summer, choked with snow and ice in winter, to hear Mass in the church at Woonsocket...."

Among the last of the parishes to be established from "The Great Milford Parish" was the one right in its own home town — Sacred Heart of Jesus, Milford — a parish that was also the first Italian-language parish established in Worcester County. Organized to serve families of artisans attracted to the Blackstone Valley by opportunities inspired by quarries in the region, Sacred Heart predated Our Lady of Mount Carmel Parish in Worcester, perhaps the most visible of the diocese's five so-called "Italian parishes" as the 21st Century approached, by a full 18 months. The first Sacred Heart Church was dedicated on Aug. 13, 1905, less than three months after Father Rocco Petrarca was named its founding

St. Theresa Church complex, East Blackstone.

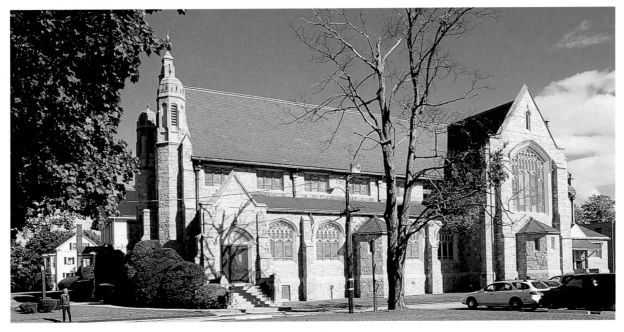

St. Mary Church, Uxbridge.

pastor. The present parish church, which has been expanded greatly in the years since its superstructure was completed after World War II, was in various stages of construction for about 21 years. During most of that time parishioners worshiped in the lower church that was roofed over and dedicated on Dec. 18,1927. Under the care of Stigmatine Fathers since 1913, Milford's Sacred Heart Parish is one of four diocesan parishes presently being cared for by religious communities, the others being St. Anne and Patrick Parish, Fiskdale (Assumptionist Fathers), St. Casimir Parish, Worcester (Marian Fathers), and St. Joseph Parish, Fitchburg, (LaSalette Fathers).

From the time he took up residence in Blackstone, Father O'Reilly celebrated Mass in Uxbridge at least once a month and purchased land on North Main Street for its first Catholic church. He had only prepared its foundation, however, when, in August of 1853, newly-ordained Father Edward J. Sheridan, was assigned as pastor of what became St. Mary Parish there. The Irish-born priest, who was raised in Canada and had practiced law before entering the seminary, finished building the simple wood frame structure that was dedicated by Bishop Fitzpatrick and served the parish for nearly 70 years, until the present church was completed in 1926. In a few

years Father Sheridan succeeded Father O'Reilly as pastor in Blackstone, but he retained Uxbridge as well — as a mission. Father Sheridan, was a "typical pioneer priest," the Uxbridge parish's centennial history claims. Whether or not that was an accurate description, the young pastor became a legendary figure in valley towns after word got around of an incident that happened early one morning as he was returning home from a midnight sick call in a neighboring town.

The story goes that Father Sheridan's carriage was stopped by three robbers intent on deviltry. Two of them, it is said, tried to enter the carriage, one from the side and one from the rear, but the fearless priest "felled one with a single blow," grabbed the other by the collar and, with his free hand, whipped the horse that ran over the third robber as it galloped away. The humbled highwayman in the priest's grasp, meanwhile, was kept restrained until being turned over to the constable in the next town. What neighboring town Father Sheridan might have been returning from that night was unknown, but it could have been almost anywhere, because in those days he had charge of the villages in Northbridge and Grafton, as well as Douglas and Sutton and even Millbury, when it reverted to mission status in 1854.

Resurrection window of St. Brigid Church, Millbury.

THE SAGA OF ST. BRIGID'S,
NÉE ST. BRIDGET'S

Perhaps no Worcester diocesan parish had a more uncertain beginning than the first one formed in the first town to which Father Fitton was called and where he is believed to have performed his first baptism: Millbury. On June 13, 1850, Father Matthew Gibson called a meeting of Catholics in the town to discuss building a church on land donated by Michael Coogan who had settled there in 1830.

Interior of St. Brigid Church, Millbury.

Work on the wood frame structure progressed rapidly because townspeople not only gave their money to the project, but their teams of oxen and mules and their labor as well — often laboring by moonlight after their own day's work was done. The first Mass was celebrated in the unpretentious church that Christmas (1850), but it was on Oct. 2, 1851, according to *The*

Pilot in Boston, that "a special train brought the bishop, 12 priests and a large number of Catholics from Worcester" for the dedication of the new edifice to St. Bridget.

The day before the dedication Bishop Fitzpatrick had appointed Father Zéphyrin Lévesque, the erstwhile pastor of French-Canadians who had just returned from his medical leave in New Orleans, to be pastor in Millbury. But he never took up residence there, opting instead to resume his residence at St. John's in Worcester and to continue ministering to French-Canadians wherever he found them, as a circuit-rider. One place where Father Lévesque did find Canadians was Spencer and, in March of 1853, he began encouraging Catholics there to build a mission church for themselves. Since resources were few, the 12 members of the community who were landowners mortgaged their homes to the church contractor. Tragically, almost immediately upon completion of the building financiers demanded that the mortgages be liquidated. A downturn in the economy made it impossible for the people to raise the funds necessary, however, and the obligated families lost their homes.

The Spencer church, which was popularly known as "St. Mary's" and which would have its own variegated history, was dedicated by Bishop Fitzpatrick on Oct. 1, 1854, and entrusted to the care of Father J. E. Napoléon Mignault who had recently been appointed pastor in Webster. Meanwhile, heartbroken by his people's plight, Father Lévesque asked to be relieved of his pastorate in order to go outside the diocese to appeal for the funds necessary to buy back the lost homes. Permissions were granted but, without a pastor, Millbury reverted to mission status, first under Uxbridge, then under St. Anne's in Worcester and later under St. Philip's in Grafton. The valiant Father Lévesque eventually did restore his people to their homes, but the effort took such a toll on his health that he was forced to leave parish ministry. He entered Gethsemane (Trappist) Abbey in Kentucky where he remained until returning to Worcester County about a year before his death in 1862.

St. Bridget was returned to parochial status in mid-1869 and flourished under that name until the early-1950s when it quietly became "St. Brigid Parish." Beginning in late-1953, the two spellings were used interchangeably in news accounts concerning the parish, most likely because about that time the pastor, Father Laurence F. O'Toole, began referring to it in correspondence as "St. Brigid." Official correspondence, too, became unpredictable. When the contract was drawn with a Boston architect for the design of a new church, rectory and youth center for the parish (the youth

Interior views of Sacred Heart of Jesus Church, Worcester.

St. Aloysius Church, sometimes known as "the church with gypsy blood," began its service as St. Mark's or St. Philip's in Grafton more than a century and one-half ago, then was moved to the Cherry Valley section of Leicester and rededicated to the patronage of St. Polycarpe. In 1869 it was moved again, to its present location atop a knoll in Leicester's Rochdale section, and again renamed. It is now a "chapel of convenience" in Rochdale's St. Aloysius-St. Jude Parish.

center was not part of the final project), for example, it was stated that "the owner (Bishop Wright) intends to erect a new St. Bridget's Church." Yet, a letter to Bishop Wright from Msgr. John F. Gannon, diocesan chancellor, dated July 2, 1954, reports "the results of the bidding (by contractors) for the St. Brigid's Parish project." Even the bishop got caught up in the jumble, for on Nov. 2, 1954, he wrote to Father O'Toole at "St. Bridget's Rectory," while on June 22, 1955, he wrote to the pastor concerning the new "St. Brigid's Church."

The invitations to the dedication of the new parish plant on Oct. 30, 1955, and the dedication booklet itself, not surprisingly, used the spelling most often associated with St. Brigid of Kildare,

the sainted nun who is patroness of Ireland, yet the spelling accepted for more than a century remained official until the publication of the 1957 edition of *The Official Catholic Directory* of the United States and Canada. That "Bridget" was the spelling intended by Bishop Fitzpatrick when he dedicated the church is clear from an entry in his journal for that day. "St. Bridget is chosen as patroness of the church," he wrote. Why that name was chosen is lost to history, but it is interesting that Father Fitton's own godmother was Bridget Keefe and that the first marriage he witnessed in Millbury, in 1833, joined one "James Gaffney" and one "Bridget Bohan" in Holy Matrimony.

It can only be speculated, too, why the spelling change was pressed because no official documentation exists — and may never have. Over the decades the predominantly-Irish parish had never had an identity problem, despite the facts that its first pastor was a Quebecer and that churchmen and historians had oftentimes spelled the names of a sainted Swedish noblewoman and the Irish nun the same way: "Bridget." Father O'Toole may have anticipated a problem, however, after some of the Millbury parish's territory was taken on July 2, 1952, in the establishment of another parish, abutting it, in the Quinsigamond Village section of Worcester. The new parish was given St. Catherine of Sweden as its patroness — an appropriate choice, given the fact that it encompassed neighborhoods where large numbers of Scandinavian, particularly Swedish,

Our Lady of Lourdes Church, Worcester.

Interior of St. Catherine of Sweden Church, Worcester.

immigrants had settled. But Father O'Toole doubtless also knew that St. Catherine of Sweden was the daughter of St. Bridget of Sweden.

When the first Mass was celebrated in Webster is also uncertain, although it is known that Father Fitton visited there as early as October of 1832. It is also likely, since Webster was not incorporated as a town until that year (1832), that the entries in Father Robert Woodley's sacramental register referring to "South Oxford" (incorporated in 1713) were actually visits to present-day Webster and included the celebration of Mass. Whatever the case, when Father Mignault was assigned to Webster on Nov. 30, 1852, to found the fifth Catholic parish in the county, he inherited an unfinished church that apparently was begun under Father Gibson's direction and was then being cared for by priests from Holy Cross College who looked after the railroaders working on the line from Worcester to Norwich and New London.

If Father George Hamilton's parish was dubbed "The Great Milford Parish," then certainly the parish Father Mignault was asked to shepherd could be called "The Great Webster Parish" for it included not only Webster but Southbridge and Spencer, Dudley, Charlton, Oxford, Leicester, the Manchaug village of Sutton, and even extended through the Brookfields to Warren and

north to New Braintree, Barre and Templeton. When Father Lévesque left the area, Father Mignault also inherited the care of French-Canadians who had begun settling in even greater numbers. Among other tasks, he encouraged the Canadians in Worcester to revive the dream of a church of their own. Accordingly, they pooled their resources and, as Richard L. Gagnon points out in his history of Notre Dame des Canadiens Parish, for $660 they purchased property on "lower Shrewsbury Street" and laid the foundation for what would eventually become St. Anne Church. On July 8, 1853, they even formed the first St. Jean Baptiste Society in Worcester in order to accumulate funds for the church's completion.

While the wood frame church that was ultimately occupied on Shrewsbury Street (as well as the Gothic-style, twin-towered, brick and granite structure that succeeded it atop Normal Hill in 1891) is often identified with the anglicized name, "St. Ann," there is little question that the first church was built by and for Worcester's French-Canadian community disenchanted with the atmosphere at St. John's and that it was dedicated to her whom Quebecers revere as "St. Anne," the grandmother of Jesus. Metallic corroboration can be found in the "St. Anne" molded in the bell that once hung in the belfry of the Normal Hill church and is now enshrined on the East Central Street lawn of the activities center of the merged Parish of Our Lady of Mount Carmel-St. Ann.

Unfortunately, the first attempts at building a church on the Shrewsbury

St. Louis Church, Webster.

Above is St. Anne Church that dominated Normal Hill in Worcester from its completion in 1891 until it was razed in 1970 after the once-thriving parish had been merged with Our Lady of Mount Carmel. The photo, right, shows the devastated church the morning after the (Sept. 21) 1938 hurricane. It was, perhaps, the most seriously damaged of all the Worcester County churches affected by the violent storm. Miraculously, the huge bell in the northern tower was not destroyed. It can be seen atop what remained of that tower (left). The towers were later reconstructed in a reconfigured form and the bell is today enshrined on the lawn of the parish center of the merged Our Lady of Mount Carmel-St. Ann Parish.

Street foundation, or of buying and moving an existing church onto it, failed. Even a later attempt by Father Gibson to erect a church there fell short when funds ran out and the unfinished structure had to be auctioned to pay mortgage obligations. In his Springfield diocesan history, Father McCoy tells of Father Gibson's going door-to-door to raise funds for his project and meeting Father Boyce who was simultaneously fund-raising for the expansion of St. John's:

"There were no parish lines then and very often the priests met in the same house or the people, frequently, while bidding Father Gibson good night and Godspeed in his work for St. Anne's, in the same breath welcomed

Father Boyce and helped him, when able, in his zealous labor for St. John's.

After health problems forced Father Gibson to take his leave of central Massachusetts early in 1856, a new era of ecclesial development evolved — with leadership from a most unlikely source.

OPPOSITE PAGE: *Detail of one of the artistic treasures of the diocese: the French-Romanesque bronze doors of Notre Dame Church, Southbridge, that contain representations of the 12 apostles and depict the 15 mysteries of the Rosary — Joyful, Sorrowful and Glorious. Blessed in 1934, there are five pairs of doors, weighing a total of 14,000 pounds. Notre Dame was the first church in Worcester County solemnly consecrated (in 1950) to perpetual service as a house of worship.*

S. JEAN   S. MATHIEU

THE ERA OF OUTREACH
TO THE COMMUNITY BEGINS

There is no clear understanding of whether Father John J. Power was sent to Worcester to be an assistant to the beloved Father Boyce or if Bishop Fitzpatrick really intended that the newly-ordained priest redeem the unfinished St. Anne Church, complete it and become shepherd of the people it would serve. The former seems more likely because Father Power had a debilitating lung problem and the bishop did not expect him to survive for any great length of time. Indeed, as John J. McGratty points out in a (1902) biography of the man the entire Worcester community affectionately came to call "Father John," the letter that Bishop Fitzpatrick sent to Father Boyce early in the summer of 1856 appointing the 27 year-old to residency on Temple Street, asked the pastor to "take good care of this young man, he will not trouble you for more than a few months at the best." What was then to begin, however, was one of the most impressive priestly careers ever in Worcester County — one that lasted not just "a few months" but almost 50 years.

Father Power, who was born in Charlestown on Aug. 23, 1828, and was a member of Holy Cross' Class of 1851, began his priestly studies in Montreal, but the severity of Quebec winters forced him to withdraw and he was reassigned to

Father John J. Power

Bishop John B. Fitzpatrick

the seminary in Aix, France, where James Augustine Healy, Holy Cross' first graduate, was already studying and where, it was hoped, the balmy breezes of the Mediterranean would help in restoring young John's health.

Ordained in France on May 17, 1856, Father Power was assigned to Worcester immediately upon his return to the United States. What the exact date was is disputed, but a plaque honoring him today in the vestibule of St. Paul Cathedral maintains that he was appointed pastor of St. Anne Parish on Aug. 6, 1856. That may well also be the day that the bishop sent him to Father Boyce, because almost from the moment of his arrival he set out to retrieve the 60-by-30 feet church skeleton on Shrewsbury Street for the 500 French-speaking Catholics then in Greater Worcester and to see its construction through to completion. With financial help from the bishop, the church was both ransomed and completed and, on Christmas Day, 1856, was dedicated with a sermon preached by Father Healy, Father Power's friend from college and seminary days — who, by the way, had recently been named chancellor of the Boston diocese and secretary to Bishop Fitzpatrick. Father Healy, who, upon his consecration as bishop of Portland (Me.) on June 2, 1875, became the first United States bishop of

St. Elizabeth Hospital, Worcester's first public hospital.

African-American ancestry, would also be the preacher when what is today St. Paul Cathedral, whose construction Father Power also directed, was dedicated on July 16, 1876.

Whether Father Power's energy was boundless and his vision unbridled or whether, at the outset, he simply intended to use the "few months" God gave him as productively as possible is, of course, a moot question. Because in the years from the time he arrived at St. John's until he died, quietly, in St. Paul Rectory on Jan. 27, 1902, Father Power, arguably, became the most eminent clergyman in all of Worcester County. He was not content in simply ministering to the people entrusted to his care in Worcester — and those in missions in Millbury and Grafton whom he attended regularly. He was an ecumenist who socialized freely with those whom he called "our separated brethren" long before that activity or that kindly description was popular, while at the same time articulating Catholic doctrine unashamedly at Mechanics Hall and championing Catholic rights fearlessly at the Statehouse. He also served the wider community as an 11-term member of the Worcester School Committee and as a board member of some of Worcester's most cherished institutions, including those of the public library and the art museum.

Perhaps his greatest contribution to the community-at-large was the sponsorship of Worcester's first public hospital — St. Elizabeth's on what was then known as Pine Street (today's Shrewsbury Street).

Worcester had a population of about 30,000 and was beginning to test its industrial mettle when, in 1864, Father Power reached out to the Religious Sisters of Mercy in New York for help in ministering to the social needs of his sprawling parish. The Sisters answered the call and on Oct. 24 that year the first five of their number — under the leadership of a daughter of a Civil War admiral — arrived to take up residence in the rectory of St. Anne Parish that the pastor had vacated and turned over to their use as a convent. Immediately the Sisters began seeking out the sick-poor in their homes and began regular visits to prisoners at the county jail and to inmates in what was then termed the "insane asylum" — the first public facility established in the United States for the care of the mentally ill, albeit one that had earned the horrified wrath of Dorothea Lynde Dix, the Worcester-based reformer of prisons, asylums and almshouses.

Sister Mary Victoria, R.S.M., and Bishop Flanagan visit at Our Lady of Mercy School.

Bishop Wright and their teachers are pictured at the first ceremony of Confirmation and First Communion for exceptional children, circa 1952, at St. Paul Cathedral.

History records that the five women who joined Father Power from New York, were the first of thousands of other women — in some 50 religious congregations — who would minister to the Catholic community and the general community of Worcester County in future decades as teachers and social workers, as housekeepers and doctors, as lawyers and administrators, as nurses and homemakers, as home health aides and spiritual directors, as women at prayer and as counter-cultural icons in times of war and weariness, in times of despair and desire, in times of fear and fury, in times of oppression and suppression.

In a 1964 brochure commemorating a centenary of service by the Sisters of Mercy to central Massachusetts, there is a recollection of their earliest days that says, in part:

"As the Sisters…undertook their journeys through the streets of the city to the homes of the needy and the sick, they found themselves to be objects of curiosity. It was not long, however, before word of their kindness and understanding spread to various parts of the city and people began to make contributions to the Sisters in the form of money, food or clothing. These gifts were rapidly put to use in the service of the poor. On their errands of mercy, the Sisters were quick to notice the social problems confronting our forefathers.…Worcester had no hospital and because so many young girls were faced with the problem of having no place to go in time of illness, Father Power approved the plan of opening St. Elizabeth's, Worcester's first public hospital."

Interior of St. Paul Cathedral as recently renovated.

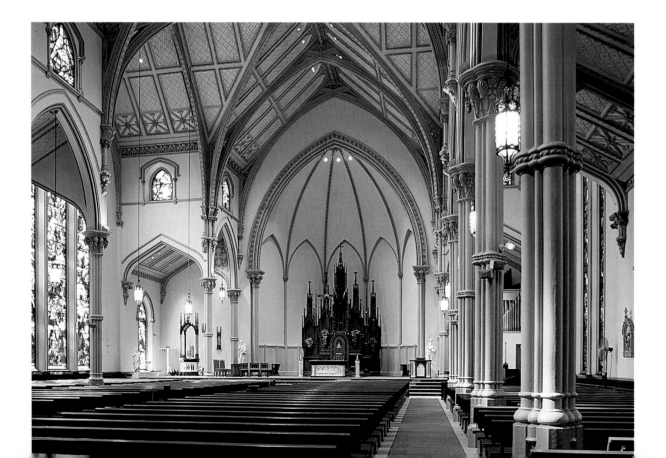

Mass following the annual pilgrimage walk on the Feast of the Assumption (Aug. 15) at the Nazareth Grotto, Leicester.

It is very possible that the 30-bed facility that was opened in a building Father Power purchased and renovated near St. Anne Church, also offered the nation's first health insurance plan, because rules stipulated that while the hospital would admit only women, the care was provided regardless of one's nationality, race or creed and that for "three dollars yearly paid when in health, one (has) a right to a bed and to all the privileges of the hospital in time of sickness." St. Elizabeth's served the community until Worcester's first City Hospital opened in 1871 on Front Street. By then, Father Power was resident near St. Paul Church, whose construction he was supervising while still shepherding St. Anne Parish.

When the new City Hospital opened and the Sisters were content that their patients would be adequately cared for, they closed St. Elizabeth Hospital and also moved to the "west side" where they soon opened an evening school for working men and women, an orphanage for girls and a hospice for working women. Eventually, too, they would open another orphanage, for boys, in Leicester. While what was known as St. Gabriel Orphanage on High Street closed in 1955, after 83 years' service to Worcester County, and St. Paul School, that was opened in 1912 under the Sisters of Mercy direction and closed in 1971 during the rash of Catholic school closings that marked that era, St. Joseph Home for Working

Women still survives on High Street and Nazareth Home still survives in Leicester as a home for dependent youngsters.

The Sisters of Mercy served with Father Power until his death in 1902. Yet, despite the reputation they have earned in Worcester County as teachers, neither St. Anne's nor St. Paul's had a parish school during his years there — this despite the fact that for many years after it was erected on June 14, 1870, he was vicar general of the eastern part of the Springfield diocese. He was not an opponent of Catholic schools, but believed strongly that Catholic students should be present in government-run schools. He was sometimes criticized for his position but it was because of his leadership that in a time of open hostility, public schools were kept open to Catholics and their non-sectarian character was confirmed. At the same time, however, Father Power preached that religious education was central to the shaping of character and life and held "catechism classes" twice a week for the children (once for adults) and encouraged the youngsters to read their catechism at home at least 15 minutes a day.

For the 11 years prior to 1869 when he moved his residence from Shrewsbury Street in order to be closer to the St. Paul construction site, the tireless Father Power was an active member of the Worcester School Committee. He did not seek election initially, but he accepted the post because he felt the children of the immigrants living in Ward Three who attended the public schools needed his voice. Also on the committee at that time was Rev. Thomas Wentworth Higginson, minister of the Free Church in Worcester who, in the mid-19th Century, was one of the young city's most militant abolitionists, an opponent of capital punishment and an outspoken proponent of women's rights and workers' rights. (Without doubt, he is best remembered in history as the Civil War colonel who commanded the 1st South Carolina Volunteers — the federal Army's first regiment of freed slaves.) It may well be that it was Father Power's close friendship with men such as Rev. Mr. Higginson, the equally-illustrious U.S. Sen. George Frisbie Hoar and Rev. William Reed Huntington, the rector of All Saints (Episcopal) Church, that caused "Father John" to be the powerful proponent that he was — in the pulpit and out — for the federal cause in the War Between the States.

When he moved from Ward 3 to Ward 7, Father Power gave up his school committee seat because he thought the new district was being well represented by a Protestant gentleman. But fair-minded people already owed him a great deal — and not just for challenging some of the petty religious prejudices that still plagued the commonwealth. One of his most celebrated victories — and one that he cherished — grew out of an incident in Grafton, sometime in 1860, after a mother and father, members of the Catholic mission that he cared for, instructed their son not to read aloud from the (Protestant) King James version of the Bible, as was the custom during opening exercises in the public schools in those days. When the boy was asked to do so one day — and refused — he was dismissed from class and then expelled by the school committee. Given the fact that Catholics were responding in great numbers to the calls to service in the Armies of both the Union and the Confederacy, Father Power believed there was a new-found sympathy for Catholics in the land and, therefore, appealed to lawmakers for relief from the Bible-reading requirement. After extensive lobbying by

Our Father's House, Fitchburg, a social service center akin to Catholic Worker houses in Worcester.

him and some central Massachusetts legislators whose help he had enlisted, on Feb. 21, 1862, the Great and General Court passed a law, by a vote of 115 to 74, that said "conscientious scruples should be a sufficient reason for relieving a teacher or a scholar from the obligation of reading the Protestant version of the Bible...."

As Catholic schools began to develop in the 1870s and 1880s, the clergy were equally as diligent in defending the rights of parents and students enrolled therein. For example, soon after St. Joseph Parish in Fitchburg opened its elementary school in 1890, Father Charles H. Jeannotte, the second pastor there, took on the Fitchburg School Board when it refused to recognize the new facility. The town had the truant officer summon one Frank Roberge to court because, as a (1965) diamond jubilee history of the parish records, "he had sent his daughter...to the parochial school for a term of 28 weeks, instead of registering her in a public school for that period."

After a trial in the Fitchburg court, Mr. Roberge was found guilty and was fined — a conviction and fine that were upheld in January of 1892 on appeal to the Superior Court in Worcester. On

Our Lady of LaSalette in St. Joseph Church, Fitchburg.

a subsequent appeal to the Supreme Judicial Court of the commonwealth, however, both the judgments against Mr. Roberge and related penalties imposed on Xavier Paulin and Anthony Leclerc were overturned when the justices ruled that parochial schools could exist as long as they, too, taught the subjects required of state schools. Father Jeannotte had not only encouraged the three parents to pursue the litigation, but personally (even though other priests offered to help) paid all their legal expenses.

SUBTLE PRESSURE
ELEVATES CATHEDRAL'S STATURE

Late in 1866, after Bishop Williams succeeded Bishop Fitzpatrick, who died on Feb. 13 that year, Father Power was asked to secure land for a new "west side" church to serve Worcester's growing Catholic population that by then numbered around 10,000. He settled on a site that at the time was a pear orchard on what was known as the "John Milton Estate," at the corner of Main Street and what was then called Corbett Street (now Chatham Street). The purchase price ($15,000) was a handsome sum in those days, but then, it was located in one of the young city's exclusive neighborhoods.

Archbishop John J. Williams

There has always been a question about why the noble, granite structure that Father Power ultimately built, was located facing a side street on the Chatham/High Streets hill, rather than on Main Street, as was originally intended. Was it really because the city needed part of the land to widen Main Street at that point, as Mayor James B. Blake insisted? Or was that simply a ruse to block its presence on the city's main thoroughfare? An article on St. Paul's in the *Worcester Telegram* of Feb. 23, 1948 — one in a continuing series on local churches — makes a blunt observation:

"Except for the plans of Mayor J.B. Blake in the late-1860s, the church would have faced Franklin Square, with a series of terraced steps leading up from Main Street. (Father Power) planned such a front when Mayor Blake told him the city wanted some of the land to widen Main Street. He warned Father Power that he had better make allowances."

Father Power apparently contemplated simply turning the building around and facing it on High Street, with its rear facing Main Street, but Bishop Williams, who tried to avoid exciting nativist tempers whenever possible, encouraged an exchange of property with abutters so that it could be constructed parallel to Main Street at the crest of the hill.

There were rumors, at the time, just before the First Vatican Council (1869-70), that Rome was

Altar boys and sanctuary choir of St. Paul Parish, Worcester, May 12, 1920. Father William H. Goggin, the pastor, is at right in bowler hat. (Photo is courtesy of Robert Raymond, then age 12, and third from left in front.)

A healing ministry that has brought attention to the Diocese of Worcester in recent years dates back at least to 1888 when a woman, reportedly bed-ridden for 16 years, was cured of dropsy during a Mass in St. Anne Church in the Fiskdale section of Sturbridge. The Shrine to St. Anne that subsequently developed there attracts thousands of pilgrims annually, particularly during the Novena leading up to the Feast of St. Anne each July (the congregation during a 1956 service is pictured above). An officially-authenticated miracle has never been claimed at the shrine, but scores of discarded canes, crutches and braces bear witness to the claim of a former rector that "prayers are heard and answered in Fiskdale." The healing ministries of (Mrs.) Eileen George of Millbury and Father Ralph DiOrio of Leicester have also drawn thousands, not only to sites in Worcester County where they have led services, but in all parts of the world where they have been invited to preach and to pray. As the new millennium dawned, the diocese was also studying claims that unusual phenomena and miraculous happenings were associated with Audrey Santo, a 16-year-old Worcester girl who has been in a coma-like state of akinetic mutism since nearly drowning in her family's above-ground swimming pool in 1987.

considering the creation of a second diocese in Massachusetts, with Worcester as its See City. Father Power, therefore, engaged the architectural firm of Eldridge Boyden, the designers of Worcester's Mechanics Hall, among other noteworthy buildings, to plan a church worthy of cathedral stature. After a successful fund-raising effort throughout the city, ground was broken in the spring of 1868 and the church's basement was completed and roofed over in time for the celebration of the first Mass there and the laying of the cornerstone for the upper church on July 4, 1869. While Bishop Williams presided at the ceremonies and was celebrant of the Mass, the revered Father

Bishop James A. Healy

The statue of the cathedral's patron, on the façade.

Fitton was invited back to the city to preach the sermon, demonstrating the solemnity of the occasion.

Father Power, who was said to have had "everything but health," nonetheless assumed the pastorate of St. Paul's at the time of those Fourth of July rites. He also continued as pastor of St. Anne Parish until Oct. 1, 1872, when he turned its care over to his associate, Father Dennis Scannell, in order to concentrate on the completion of the Gothic-style superstructure of St. Paul's. Except for its graceful, 145-feet-tall bell tower that was added in 1889, the church that eventually would be a cathedral was completed and solemnly dedicated on July 16, 1876 — 100 years, almost to the day, after Isaiah Thomas, Worcester's patriot-printer, read the Declaration of Independence for the first time in New England from a porch on the town's meetinghouse on the Common, a couple of blocks away. Presiding at

St. Paul's dedication was now-Archbishop Williams who, on Feb.12, 1875, had acceded to Boston's designation as an archdiocese, and preaching was Father Power's old friend, now-Bishop James A. Healy of Portland. Performing the actual dedication, however, was Bishop Patrick T. O'Reilly, the pastor of neighboring St. John Parish who, on June 24, 1870, had been named the first bishop of Springfield, a diocese encompassing the five counties of central and western Massachusetts. The rumors were accurate. Rome had been contemplating a new diocese for Massachusetts. Only the speculation concerning the See City was incorrect — even though Worcester and particularly the mother church, St. John's, played a signally important role during its formative years.

The stained glass windows that adorned St. Paul's after its completion — including the 52-feet-high windows that enlivened the east and west transepts

— were done by Samuel West of Boston, one of the nation's earliest glass craftsmen. According to his (1891) obituary, the original transept windows, which depicted the birth, death and resurrection of Jesus, were considered the largest windows created in the United States to that time. They, together with the Italian marble statue of St. Paul that still occupies a niche on the cathedral's façade above the main portico, were gifts to the parish from the family of George Crompton, the loom maker (who, with the possible exception of the incomparable Robert H. Goddard, held more patents than any mechanic in Worcester County history), and his wife, Mary. During a renovation of the cathedral in the early-1960s, new windows depicting the life and teachings of its patron, designed by Clare Leighton, a Connecticut wood engraver making her first venture into the medium of stained glass, were installed by Bishop Bernard J. Flanagan, the second bishop of Worcester. The new windows, striking for their blazing reds and stunning blues, had been commissioned by Bishop Wright before he was transferred to the Diocese of Pittsburgh in 1959, in the belief that the building should have windows "proportionate in their quality to the dignity of the church as a cathedral and to the beauty of the design and appointments of St. Paul's…."

Toward the end of the 1960s, as liturgical reforms initiated by the Second Vatican Council were being

The window depicting the execution of St. Paul in St. Paul Cathedral.

implemented, the cathedral was again extensively renovated. This time, in keeping with the Council's call for simpler liturgical settings lest the worshipers' attention be distracted from the central reenactment taking place at the altar, the ornate, multi-spired, white marble-faced main altar and reredos were removed from the rear wall of the sanctuary and replaced, as was the case over a period of time in other diocesan churches and chapels, with a free-standing altar centered in the sanctuary.

Also removed from the cathedral sanctuary at that time, however, — and replaced by a simple "presider's chair" behind the high altar — was the majestic throne on which Bishop Wright and, later, Bishop Flanagan were seated when they liturgically assumed jurisdiction in the Diocese of Worcester.

Sadly, the chair that gave meaning to the episcopal throne installed on March 6, 1950, was lost when the throne was ruthlessly dismembered during the late-1960s' renovations.

Opposite page: The west transept windows of St. Paul Cathedral (with its 52-feet-high center lancet) portray the main pattern of events in the life of St. Paul, the cathedral's patron, up to the time of his conversion. The artist, Clare Leighton, calls this the "Oriental Window." The events in the east transept windows depict the apostle's later ministry against a Mediterranean background.

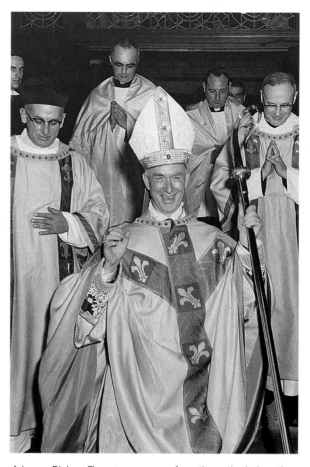

A happy Bishop Flanagan emerges from the cathedral on the day of his installation, Sept. 24, 1959. His chaplains were Very Rev. William A. Donaghy, S.J., left, president of Holy Cross College, and Very Rev. Armand H. Desautels, A.A., president of Assumption College.

The original episcopal throne in St. Paul Cathedral.

Gone, too — perhaps forever, as far as public reverence is possible — were the wood carvings of SS. Oswald and Wulstan of Old World Worcester and the other adornments that made the throne the period treasure that it was. Happily, the location of the chair was traced to the sanctuary of a church in Greater Boston that had, somehow, acquired it and, prior to the installation of Bishop Timothy J.

Harrington as the third bishop of Worcester on Oct. 13, 1983, arrangements were made for it to be "borrowed" for use at those rites in Worcester's Memorial Auditorium. Before Bishop Daniel P. Reilly was installed as the diocese's fourth Ordinary on Dec. 8, 1994, however, Father John J. Bagley, a former diocesan chancellor who coordinated all events celebrating the diocese's silver and golden anniversaries during the Jubilee Years of 1975 and 2000, negotiated for the permanent return of the chair. It was then used at Bishop Reilly's installation and, when the most recent renovations to the cathedral were carried out in 1996, it was again placed permanently in the sanctuary as the bishop's chair behind the high altar.

THE NATION'S
OLDEST PARISH CHURCH

Springfield (1870) was the fifth Catholic diocese to be established in New England. Besides Boston (1808) and Hartford (1843), Portland and Burlington had been created in 1853. By the time they left the embrace of the Archdiocese of New York in 1875 (raised to archdiocesan stature in 1850) to be reorganized as part of the newly-designated Archdiocese of Boston, Providence (1872), too, had joined the rolls of (arch)dioceses in the Universal Church. Later, Manchester (1884), Fall River (1904) and Worcester (1950) would be established as separate dioceses before Hartford was given archdiocesan stature (1953), with Bridgeport and Norwich being created and (along with Providence) being designated as suffragan dioceses in the new Church province.

Father Patrick T. O'Reilly was still three months away from his 37th birthday when he was consecrated a bishop on Sept. 25, 1870, by New York's Archbishop John McCloskey in St. Michael Cathedral in Springfield. Among those in attendance were about 600 people who had boarded a special train from Worcester that

A commemoration of Bishop Patrick T. O'Reilly at the entrance to St. John Church, Worcester.

In Memoriam

Rt. Rev.
PATRICK T. O'REILLY D. D.
First Bishop of Springfield,
former Pastor of this Church.
Born Dec. 24, 1833,
Ordained Priest Aug. 15, 1857,
Consecrated Bishop Sept. 25, 1870,
Died May 28, 1892.
R. I. P.

morning. They included many parishioners of "old St. John's" on Temple Street, where the new bishop was — and would remain — pastor.

The diocese that Bishop O'Reilly was called upon to shepherd included an estimated 100,000 people, 38 parish churches and about 14 missions, 43 priests, two parochial schools, 12 Sisters, one college and one orphanage.

Eighteen of the parishes were in Worcester County, including seven established (or, in the case of St. Bridget's in Millbury, reestablished) in just the previous year. Several of the parishes, including St.

Top of the page: *the Last Supper window in Our Lady of the Lake Church, Leominster.*

St. Michael Cathedral, Springfield.

Immaculate Conception Church in Lancaster, the eldest town in Worcester County.

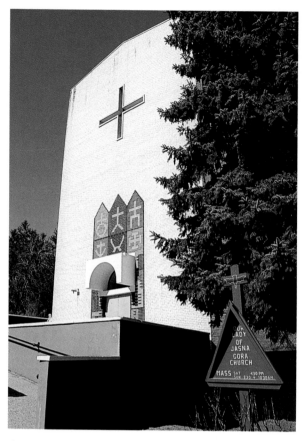

Our Lady of Jasna Gora Church, Clinton.

John's in Clinton that Father O'Reilly had served from St. John's in Worcester when he was a curate there from 1857 to 1862, were already occupying their second church building (or in the case of St. Bernard's in Fitchburg, the third).

Father Matthew Gibson is believed to have celebrated the first Mass in what was then the Clintonville section of Lancaster in 1845 and traveled to the village at least every two months for the next two years until turning its care over to Father John Boyce who, not long thereafter, was making the trek from Worcester once-a-week. At first the sanctuary was in the home of a parishioner or in a mill house owned by the Bigelow Carpet Co. But in 1849 Father Boyce encouraged the people to begin thinking about building their own church. They did, and on Oct. 4, 1850, a 250-seat church that was later doubled in size was dedicated. The village remained a mission of St. John's in Worcester until it was given parochial status on Dec. 1, 1862. Father Richard J. Patterson directed the construction of

both the second, considerably larger, wood frame church on Pleasant Street, in 1869, and the present Romanesque St. John Church that Bishop O'Reilly dedicated on June 27, 1886.

Also among the newer parishes Bishop O'Reilly inherited were St. Martin's in Otter River, St. Peter's (now St. Mary's) and Notre Dame in Southbridge, St. Joseph's in North Brookfield, St. Paul's and Notre Dame des Canadiens' in Worcester, St. Philip's in Grafton, St. Luke's (later St. Anthony's and still later Our Lady of Good Counsel) in West Boylston and Sacred Heart in Webster.

Otter River and Athol, unquestionably, were the farthest mission outposts served by priests from St. John's in Worcester. After establishing the first formal mission of Worcester with the construction of "the shanty cathedral" for Fitchburg Catholics in 1848, Father Gibson organized two outmissions for that mission. He celebrated the first Mass in the small church he built in Templeton's Otter River section in 1854, and the following year he celebrated the first

Mass in the former Baptist church he had renovated for use by Athol's Catholic community. From the time St. Bernard's became a parish in 1856, until Otter River was separated from it eight years later, both Otter River and Athol, along with Leominster, were missions of Fitchburg. But in 1864 St. Catherine of Siena Mission, as the church in Athol was known, was attached to St. Martin's. Simultaneously priests in Otter River were assigned responsibility for Catholics in Orange, Petersham, Westminster, Royalston, Hubbardston, Ashburnham, Barre and Gardner.

While the railroads cutting through northern and western Worcester County stimulated the first great Catholic migration to the region (Father Gibson is said to have found "300 railroad men" in Royalston in 1846), Father Fitton's diary records Masses in Templeton as early as 1837. The region was not slumbering before then, though. Indeed, Barre, for one, was a thriving stagecoach junction that was sometimes called "the Gateway to the Western Frontier." It boasted as many as seven hostelries in the 1830s, and, as Gabrielle Healy Carroll wrote melodically in a history of St. Joseph Parish in 1996, Barre was "the bustling prosperous hub of a cluster of small villages that had grown up north of Worcester."

Among other mission churches that Bishop O'Reilly inherited upon his installation in 1870 were St. Mary's in Brookfield that was being served by priests from the recently-established (1867) St. Joseph Parish in North Brookfield and two that had been built by Father Thomas

F. Griffin, the bishop's associate at St. John's, and were attached to the mother church — St. Mary's in Holden Center that then-Father O'Reilly had dedicated two years earlier upon designation by Bishop Williams, and St. Joseph's in Auburn that he had been deputed to dedicate the previous Thanksgiving Day.

The Church in Brookfield is one of 20 former Protestant or Episcopal churches that were

St. Mary Church, Brookfield, that traces its lineage to the Brookfield Massacre of 1675, may well be "the oldest parish building still being used by Roman Catholics in all the vast territory settled by the English in North America." Much of the building dates from 1717 — 15 years before George Washington was born — while the tower and belfry date from 1789, the year Gen. Washington became the nation's first President and the year John Carroll became the nation's first Catholic bishop.

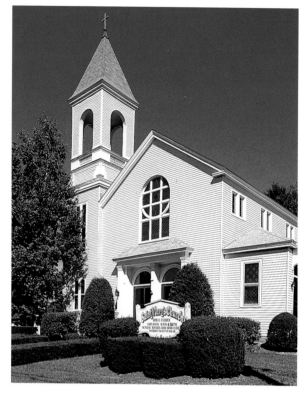

St. Mary Church, Jefferson.

acquired and renovated for use by Worcester County Catholics over the years. But it is special. Indeed, some might argue that no church building of whatever heritage, size or architectural design — perhaps no building of any kind — in central Massachusetts is as noteworthy as that building that traces its lineage to the Brookfield Massacre of 1675.

According to Robert W. Wilder, Brookfield's unofficial town historian in the late-20th Century, the original sections of what is now St. Mary Church date from 1717 when Brookfield's second meetinghouse was constructed in the general locale where the first had stood before being destroyed in the Aug. 2 to 5, 1675, siege of the town by a hostile force of Native Americans led by Wampanoag sachem Metacomet (King Philip), the renegade son of Chief Massasoit who had befriended the Pilgrims at Plymouth. The original site of the meetinghouse in what was organized as Quaboag Plantation was about where Foster Hill in West Brookfield is located today, but at that time — only two years after Brookfield's incorporation as a town — it was near the

geographic center of the settlement that now comprises several towns. Construction of the original post-and-beam building had only just been completed when it and all the homes and barns and other outbuildings of the 12 families in the settlement were burned. With eight dead and five wounded and hostiles still rampaging throughout central and eastern Massachusetts, the General Court in Boston ordered the entire settlement abandoned.

Resettlement was authorized in 1686, but it would be another 30 years before there were enough frontier families on the plantation to again warrant the construction of a meetinghouse. The replacement structure that was completed in 1717 was, like its predecessor and all other town meetinghouses in those by-gone days, both the political center of the settlers' lives as well as their gathering place as members of the established (Congregational) Church.

In 1747, at the time of the death of Rev. Thomas Cheney who had served the place since 1717, a long-simmering debate erupted between settlers in the town's western and eastern districts over whether to build a larger meetinghouse. It continued until 1754 when the Foster Hill structure was taken down by some of the community's frustrated members and reassembled near where the Brookfield Town Common is

Our Lady, Queen of Heaven Mission, Royalston, the town where Empress Zita and other members of the deposed Austrian-Hungarian Court of the Holy Roman Empire summered throughout the years of World War II and in the post-war years. They worshiped in pews reserved for them at Our Lady Immaculate Church, Athol.

The interior of St. Joseph Church, Barre.

located today. When an appeal of the clandestine move to the General Court by distraught settlers of the western district failed, an entirely new religious society was formed there.

Improvements were made to the relocated building over the next several years and in 1789 — the year George Washington was inaugurated as the nation's first President and the year Father John Carroll was confirmed as the nation's first Roman Catholic bishop — a steeple, with a belfry, was added. In 1828, Mr. Wilder said, Unitarians replaced the Congregationalists as the dominant religious body in town and acquired all of their assets — including the then-111-year-old meetinghouse that had been moved to the Common. In 1849, a consortium of local residents purchased the structure, Mr. Wilder explained, and moved it directly across River Street to the lot where the present stone Unitarian church stands. The consortium immediately began renting the basement of the building to the town for government meetings and its gathering rooms were made available for social functions. By the 1850s Catholics, who were arriving in great numbers to work in the town's shoe and boot factories, began renting space for worship services.

Finally, in 1865, two years before St. Joseph's was established in North Brookfield as the first Catholic parish in that part of Worcester County, Father William Moran, pastor of All Saints Parish in Ware, purchased the hallowed Brookfield structure for conversion into a Catholic mission

church and moved it yet another time to the lot he had purchased on Lincoln Street, where it still stands — in its 283rd year, in its fourth location, serving its third religious denomination. It became the gathering place for a separate Catholic parish community in 1885.

What is now St. Mary Church has, naturally, undergone expansion and extensive renovation over the years. But, according to Mr. Wilder, the frame, floor joists, roof rafters and much of the wall and roof sheathing have survived since 1717. Most of the church's major beams are of hewn American chestnut, but the addition of some white oak was necessitated by one or another of the building's three moves — first by Congregationalists, then by Unitarians and, finally, by Roman Catholics. While there has been speculation that some of the materials used in the construction of the second meetinghouse (and, therefore, of the present St. Mary's) may have been salvaged from the building destroyed in 1675

The window depicting the parish's patron in St. Aloysius Gonzaga Church, Gilbertville.

The exterior and interior of St. John Church, Worcester, the mother church of two dioceses.

by King Philip's warriors, such claims may never be authenticated.

Nevertheless, the place of St. Mary's in the folklore of central Massachusetts is secure. There is no question that it is the oldest parish building being used for Catholic worship in the region. Additionally, Mr. Wilder maintained, it may be "the oldest parish building still being used by Roman Catholics in all the vast territory settled by the English in North America."

Such speculation was not contravened by research done recently for the Worcester diocesan history project by Jane Devine, architecture/art librarian at the University of Notre Dame. She found that several colonial-era chapels in Maryland were still being used, but none that dated earlier than 1727 (Doughoregan Manor in Howard County, Md.). St. Mary Chapel in St. Mary's City, Md., built in the 1630s, was the first Catholic church built in the colonies by the English, but it does not survive. The Archdiocese of Washington, within whose present-day boundaries Jesuit Father Andrew White celebrated the first Catholic Mass in the colonies in 1634, also includes St. Francis Xavier Parish in Newtowne, Md., that dates from 1640. Its parish church, however, which the Washington archdiocese identifies as "the oldest Catholic church in the original 13 colonies," dates only from 1731.

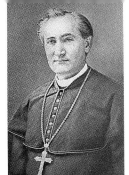

A "CO-CATHEDRAL"
AND WORCESTER'S FIRST CHANCERY

Bishop O'Reilly, who was born in County Cavan, Ireland, on Christmas Eve of 1833, studied for the priesthood in Maryland and was ordained in Boston on the Feast of the Assumption, 1857, was immediately assigned as an assistant to Father Boyce at St. John's in Worcester. He was reassigned to Boston in 1862 as pastor of St. Joseph Parish in the West End, but served there for only two years — until returning to St. John's, as pastor, upon the death of Father Boyce. The bishop did not immediately sever his ties to St. John's after being named the first bishop of Springfield. In fact, he retained both his residence there and his title as pastor of the parish, while naming his curate, Father Griffin, then ordained only three years, rector of the church and chancellor of the diocese, in effect, designating the parish house of St. John's as the Chancery of the infant diocese seated 50 miles away. To assure peace of mind concerning Springfield, the young bishop named another friend, the "energetic and inspiring" Father James J. McDermott, at the time pastor of St.

Peter's in Southbridge, to be the first rector of the newly-designated St. Michael Cathedral.

The bishop had offered the cathedral post to Father William A. Power, then serving with his brother, John, at St. Paul's in Worcester, but he declined the honor, preferring instead to become pastor in Blackstone. Shortly, the bishop named Father John Power to be vicar general of the eastern region of the new diocese, an office he held into the years of Bishop Thomas D. Beaven's tenure as second bishop of Springfield. Upon Bishop O'Reilly's death, on May 28, 1892, Pope Leo XIII confirmed Archbishop John Williams' appointment of Father Power as administrator of the diocese, a post he held until Bishop Beaven's consecration on Oct. 18, 1892.

Letters from Archbishop John J. Williams appointing Father John J. Power administrator of the Springfield diocese, following the death of Bishop O'Reilly, and from Pope Leo XIII confirming the appointment.

TOP OF THE PAGE: *Bishop Patrick T. O'Reilly*

89

Interestingly, Bishop O'Reilly's decision to serve Springfield from Worcester was not unprecedented. Hartford's Bishop Tyler, of course, had served all of Connecticut and Rhode Island from ecclesial offices he established in Providence. But closer to home, Father George Reardon, sometimes described as "a native of Worcester," who was appointed "the first pastor of Springfield" in 1840, never took up residence there but opted instead to serve it and other missions entrusted to him from the small home he maintained on Park (now Franklin) Street in Worcester, not too far from Christ Church. It was from there that in 1846 he negotiated the purchase of a Baptist meetinghouse that, under the patronage of Our Lady and St. Benedict, became Springfield's first Catholic church. Shortly, however, it would evolve into what, in 1870, became St. Michael Cathedral. It is in the crypt of St. Michael's that Bishop O'Reilly is buried.

St. John's, of course, was never officially given the title of "co-cathedral," but Bishop O'Reilly was not timid about having the spotlight shine on his own parish church. For example, the first ordination ceremony for the Springfield diocese was held at St. John's, on April 29, 1871, when the bishop ordained Daniel Shiel and Michael Carroll, both natives of Ireland, to priesthood. Father Shiel, whom Bishop O'Reilly lists as the first priest he ordained, was immediately assigned to Fitchburg and given the care of its mission in Leominster, St. Leo's. On Jan. 2, 1873, he was named founding pastor of that parish, a community he continued to serve for more than 30 years.

Bishop Thomas D. Beavan

Bishop Thomas M. O'Leary

St. Leo's, incidentally, is one of two diocesan parishes whose members worshiped in two separate Protestant churches in their earliest years. The Baptist church that Father Gibson had purchased in 1852, was succeeded by a former Methodist church that served the Leominster community from 1866 until the present church was completed in 1900. In Worcester, members of Notre Dame des Canadiens Parish worshiped in a former Methodist church and later in a former Baptist church before their present church was completed in 1929.

Worcester's St. John's was also the site of the ordination to subdiaconate of the founding pastor of historic St. Joseph Parish in Webster — the mother parish not only of the seven Polish-language parishes in Worcester County, but of all Polish-language parishes in New England. There has long been confusion over when the Webster parish's first church was completed and when the first pastor was assigned. However, according to Father Richard F. Meehan, archivist of the Diocese of Springfield, Bishop O'Reilly's journal leaves no doubt about the ordination date of the young man who assumed the Webster pastorate on the day of his ordination to priesthood, May 21, 1888.

It appears that the first, wood frame, church of St. Joseph Parish was nearing completion when Bishop O'Reilly contacted SS. Cyril and Methodius Seminary in Michigan, inquiring whether a Polish-speaking priest was available to assume the pastorate in Webster. While the seminary has no record of the correspondence today, legend has it that Father Francis S. Chalupka, often described as "a Polish-speaking Czech," was recommended to Bishop O'Reilly — upon payment of an outstanding tuition bill of $600 by the "70 families and several single individuals" who would comprise the original parish population. A hand-written entry in the bishop's journal for May 6, 1888, records that "this morning while I was saying Mass (at St. John's), Mr. Francis Chalupka arrived. I intend to ordain him in a few days for the Polish Catholics of the diocese. I think he will be the first Polish priest ordained for New England." Later journal entries, Father Meehan pointed out, show that the bishop ordained the young man to the order of subdeacon at St. John's

Interior and exterior of St. Joseph Basilica, Webster.

on May 17, 1888, to the diaconate on the following day at St. Michael Cathedral, and to priesthood, also at St. Michael's, on Pentecost Monday (May 21).

While it is reported that immediately upon his ordination Father Chalupka boarded a train for Webster to make himself available to hear the Confessions of his new parishioners, the young man did not offer his "first Mass," a celebration that was also the first Mass offered in the yet-to-be-completed St. Joseph Church, until the following Sunday, Trinity Sunday, May 27, 1888. It appears that the completed church was dedicated by Bishop O'Reilly during the summer of 1889, while the present parish church, which was raised to the dignity of a minor basilica on Oct. 11, 1998, was completed in 1914. At the time of its designation as a basilica by Pope John Paul II, it was said to have been only the 36th church so honored in the United States.

Bishop O'Reilly relinquished the pastorate of St. John's in 1885, entrusting its care to his long-time associate, Father Griffin. But the bishop's devotion to the mother church continued right up to his death seven years later at the age of 58.

During Bishop O'Reilly's years as Ordinary of the diocese, the number of parishes in Worcester County grew to 48 — 21 of them having been established in the decade of the 1880s alone — and a number of

The former Fox Mills factory building at Worcester's Kelley Square that housed the church and school and rectory of St. Anthony Parish from the time it was founded as a mission in 1895 until it was suppressed as a parish in 1975.

St. Anne Mission in Dana that was lost, as the entire town was lost, when construction of the Quabbin Reservoir caused the inundation of the Swift River Valley. Dana and three Hampshire county towns ceased to exist on April 27, 1938.

mission churches that would later become parishes also flourished. Under Bishop Beaven, who died on Oct. 5, 1920, after 28 years as head of the diocese, and Bishop Thomas M. O'Leary, Springfield's third bishop, who served until his death on Oct. 10, 1949, a total of 49 additional parishes were added to Worcester County's parochial roster. In that same time period, two parishes that had previously held parochial status — St. Matthew's in the Cordaville section of Southboro and St. Peter's in Petersham — reverted to mission status, St. Matthew's reversing roles with its former mission, St. Anne's in Southboro Center, and St. Peter's returning to the embrace of its mother parish, Our Lady Immaculate, Athol.

Both St. Matthew's and St. Peter's would be restored to parish stature after the Diocese of Worcester was established, but another mission that thrived during many of those years between 1892 and 1950 would not survive.

A few formerly independent parishes in the 60 towns and cities now part of the Worcester diocese have been merged or "twinned" with neighboring parishes over the years and three have been suppressed — St. Anthony's, the so-called "factory church" in Worcester's Kelley Square neighborhood, and Our Lady of the Rosary and St. Mary's, both in Spencer, that were united on New Year's Day, 1994, as Mary, Queen of the Rosary Parish. Many other parishes have undergone one or more name changes. But no Catholic church or chapel hereabouts is more defunct than St. Anne's in Dana because not only was the 125-seat, gray, clapboard mission church razed in the late-summer of 1938 as engineers proceeded with the creation of the Quabbin Reservoir, but, in fact, virtually the entire Town of Dana was inundated and the chapel's congregation was dispersed. Established in January of 1904 as a mission of Our Lady Immaculate Parish, Athol, the tiny "chapel on the hill," as it was

St. Matthew Church, Southboro.

St. Anne Church, Southboro.

sometimes called because of its commanding view of the entire North Dana area, was dedicated on May 13, 1907. It remained a mission of the Athol parish except for the years 1917 to 1933 when St. Peter's in Petersham first had parochial status and Dana, which abutted it, 12 miles south of Athol, was assigned to it as a mission. Dana was a thriving Worcester County town of small farms and factories and stores. But it, along with the Towns of Enfield, Greenwich and Prescott, in Hampshire County, legally ceased to exist at midnight on April 27, 1938, 11 years after the Great and General Court enacted the legislation that authorized the taking by eminent domain of some 39 square miles of land in the Swift River Valley in the construction of Greater Boston's newest source of drinking water.

Near the turn of the 20th Century when earlier land-takings produced the Wachusett Reservoir, also to help quench the thirst of residents of eastern Massachusetts, Catholic church buildings in West Boylston and Boylston were displaced and the cemetery of St. John Parish in Clinton had to be relocated. But at least the better part of those towns survived and their names remain on maps of the commonwealth. Not so with Dana.

Following the first celebration of "Soil Stewardship Sunday" in the diocese, on a farm in Oxford, in 1956, participating members of the diocesan Council of Catholic Youth erected 98 wayside shrines in all corners of the county as part of "Operation Crossroads," a joint effort of the CYC and the Diocesan Rural Life Apostolate. The small, roofed crucifixes some of which still exist, were placed on private property near major highway intersections to remind passersby on the interconnection of rural and urban life in central Massachusetts and the world.

A SCHOOL SYSTEM
IS FIRMLY ESTABLISHED

During Bishop O'Reilly's tenure as bishop, too, a county-wide Catholic school system — which had as its earliest models the school conducted by Father Fitton on Mount St. James and others conducted by lay people in Notre Dame Parish, Southbridge, and at St. Bernard's in Fitchburg — was well underway with 19 elementary schools and two high schools functioning at the time of his death. The number would swell to 73 parish, diocesan and private elementary and high schools as the 1964-65 academic year was getting underway. Attrition in subsequent years was severe, however, so that by the autumn of 1987 only ten parish, diocesan and private high schools and 23 parish, regional, diocesan and private elementary schools were open. One reason for the closings was that religious communities were unable to continue providing the level of staffing of earlier years — or, in some cases, to supply any teachers at all. That fact inevitably led to higher tuitions as lay teachers succeeded their consecrated counterparts in the classrooms. Perhaps more significantly, though, a crisis of confidence set in as questions of the schools' continued "Catholicity," without Religious teachers, were raised.

"It is easy to identify the nature of a school when a dozen or more Sisters are living in the convent next door," Bishop Flanagan once said, adding "it is

The first Catholic School Board met for the first time on March 6, 1969, at Holy Name High School. Members were, from left, Dr. Helen G. Vassallo, James J. Marshall, Brother J. Conal Owens, C.F.X., Bishop Flanagan, Auxiliary Bishop Harrington, Sister Rolande St. Jean, S.A.S.V., and Paul V. Mullaney; standing are Rev. John D. Thomas, Sister Mary Charlene, S.S.C., Sister Christina Maria, S.S.J., Msgr. Edmund G. Haddad, Msgr. Stanislaus J. Kubik, Rev. Raymond J. Page, Rev. John J. Foley, Miss Mary J. McDermott, J. Gregory O'Neill, Sister Mary Cecilia, R.S.M., and Sister Mary Angeline, P.B.V.M. Absent was Michael J. Morrill.

less easy when commitment is not clothed in a religious habit." But the essence of a Catholic school, he said "is in the philosophy that nurtures it and the understanding administrators and teachers have of the responsibilities imposed by their own Baptism, not on whether the principal or the teacher is ordained or consecrated in religious life."

Other factors, of course, contributed to the school-closing frenzy of the 1970s. After all, the allure of nationality-based schools had been severely compromised by the growing acceptance of inter-ethnic marriages and the post-World War II migration of young families away from traditional ethnic neighborhoods. It should be remembered that when the Diocese of Worcester was established in 1950, fully 32 of the 60 schools that were amalgamated into the diocesan school system were foreign language-driven. They had not only helped to ease several generations of children into English-speaking American life but played an essential role in the desire of immigrants to preserve and pass on the cultures of their native lands.

For Lithuanians and Poles and Slovaks and Italians who, with the Irish and French-Canadians comprised most of the early Catholic immigration hereabouts, preservation of language and culture — as with most later immigration — was both a practical and emotional exercise. But for French-Canadian settlers who suffered under English oppression for generations in Quebec and the Maritime Provinces — and who, in 1950, supported 22 parish schools in Worcester County, as well as Assumption College and High School — preserving language had a theological significance. For them, "Qui perd sa langue perd sa foi!" (he who loses his language loses his faith!) was akin to an 11th commandment.

By the 1970s, too, autocratic pastors who in earlier days might have denied the Sacraments to parents who sent their children to the public schools were pretty much only a bad memory. In fact, well before then Catholics had come to feel very much at home in the public schools — there was even a diocesan-wide guild of public school teachers (the Guild of the Holy Spirit)!

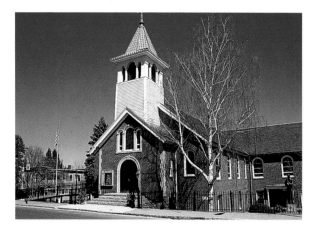

St. Anthony di Padua Church, Fitchburg.

Interior of St. Francis of Assisi Church, Fitchburg.

Former high altar of St. Francis of Assisi Church, Athol.

A sign of the times: the steeple of St. John Church, Worcester, as seen through the ruins of the 86-year-old former school as it was being torn down during the summer of 1977.

Whatever the causes, Bishop Flanagan often said the greatest heartache of his 24 years as head of the Diocese of Worcester was presiding over the closing of so many schools. "In some instances I think we acted too hastily," he lamented.

The actual peak of the Worcester diocesan enrollment graph, according to official school department records, was in 1960-61 when 26,431 students were registered, county-wide. The figure remained near or above 25,000 students through the decade of the 1960s, but

Sisters from throughout the diocese are pictured during a general session of a 1950s' Diocesan Teachers' Convention in Worcester's Memorial Auditorium.

the decline that accompanied the 1970s' school closings continued until the 1990-91 academic year when a low point of 9,123 children and young adults were enrolled in the school system.

While in earlier years no fewer than 14 Worcester County parishes sponsored both an elementary school and a four-year high school, as the Third Millennium dawned only one of the diocese's 126 parishes — Our Lady of Czestochowa, Worcester — had a kindergarten through Grade 12 program. Still, the striking comparative portraits of the school system that was being organized in 1950 and the one that existed as the 1999-2000 academic year began, were heartening. In 1950, official records show, 20,653 young people were being instructed by 635 Sisters and Brothers and three lay teachers (a student-teacher ratio of 32-to-one), while as the 20th Century gave way to the 21st, the 10,293 young people enrolled in Worcester County's 33 Catholic schools were being instructed by 51 priests, Sisters and Brothers and 622 lay men and lay women (a ratio of 15-to-one). Equally as important in a Church committed to a Gospel that propounds social justice, the "stipends" that were accorded to Religious teachers in earlier years had been replaced by salaries arrived at, in many instances, through collective bargaining.

LEFT AND OPPOSITE PAGE: Our Lady of Czestochowa Church, and icon, Worcester.

A major contributor to the early vitality of the Catholic school system was St. John's Msgr. Griffin (he was named a monsignor in 1889) whose invitations to the Sisters of Notre Dame de Namur, the Irish Christian Brothers and, later, the Xaverian Brothers gave birth to the first parish schools in the City of Worcester. They, along with members of the Society of Jesus and the Worcester-based Sisters of Mercy, were among the religious communities that generously invested their personnel in Worcester County schools over the years. Others have included the Sisters of St. Joseph (Holyoke), the Fitchburg-based Sisters of the Presentation of the Blessed Virgin Mary, Sisters of St. Anne (Marlboro), Sisters of the Assumption (Nicolet), Gray Nuns of Montreal, Sisters of the Presentation of Mary, Sisters of the Holy Cross of the Seven Dolors, Faithful Companions of Jesus, Daughters of the Holy Spirit, Sisters of St. Felix of Cantalice, Franciscan Sisters of St. Joseph, Sisters of St. Casimir, Sisters of the Holy Family of Nazareth, Daughters of Our Lady of Mercy, Religious Venerini Sisters, Bernardine Sisters, School Sisters of St. Francis, Brothers of the Sacred Heart and Assumptionist Fathers.

Msgr. Griffin, whom contemporaries called "a war horse for the faith," was also responsible for inviting the Sisters of Providence to take up residence in central Massachusetts and to open a home for the aged. In fact, they founded St. Vincent Hospital, the only Catholic hospital in Worcester County that, with its related Providence House nursing homes in

The original (1890s) St. Vincent Hospital and its (1950s) successor atop Worcester's Union Hill.

Worcester, Millbury and Southbridge, continues today, albeit with little direct involvement of the Sisters.

The hospital, which in the 1960s boasted of more than 600 beds and was the second largest private hospital in medically-astute Massachusetts, is now part of the Worcester Medical Center complex that opened in early-2000 on reclaimed land in downtown Worcester. While its principal owner is Tenet Healthcare Corp. of Santa Barbara, Calif., and it had become a for-profit enterprise, St. Vincent's remained a hospital "operated according to Catholic ethical standards," local administrators maintained. The diocese had negotiated a "covenant agreement" to that effect with physicians and others connected with Fallon Community Health Plan who assumed ownership of the hospital in the late-1980s. (It should not go unsaid that in the mid-to-late-1990s, when the quality and the delivery of health care in the United States was undergoing intensive scrutiny and dramatic change, the health plan that originated with the predominantly-Catholic physicians and nurses, researchers and technicians affiliated with St. Vincent's and "the Fallon Clinic" was judged by two respected evaluators of such matters — *Newsweek* and *U.S. News and World Report* magazines — as "the best" Health Maintenance Organization in the nation.)

98

EARLIER MINISTRIES
REVISITED

For about five years, early in the 20th Century, The Sisters of Providence also operated Mount St. Joseph Home, "a maternity hospital for unfortunate young women," on a satellite campus in Millbury. However, on Aug. 16, 1920, the Sisters' archives remember, "fire broke out in the attic" of its principal building and it was destroyed, the staff and the 15 women and the five babies they were caring for at the time being transferred to St. Vincent's. The hospital corporation considered rebuilding there, but after about four years the plan was scuttled because Millbury was "too far removed from the city." Meanwhile, the hospital on Union Hill, together with the men and women connected with the child care programs the Sisters sponsored through St. Agnes Guild redoubled their efforts in behalf of the "unfortunate young women" and all other women and children who approached them for care. On Nov. 4, 1956, a public witness so nobly begun in 1915 amid the farmland of Millbury, was resurrected, however, when a home on Winthrop Street was blessed by Bishop Wright and opened, unashamedly, indeed, proudly, as "a home for unwed mothers."

Known simply as "Marillac Manor," the hospice was dedicated to St. Louise de Marillac, a companion of St. Vincent de Paul after whom the hospital directly across the street was named. When it closed its doors in 1988 it was not for lack of commitment. Rather, as with other charitable works of the Church that have changed as the times have demanded, officials of the

diocesan Bureau of Catholic Charities said that as the stigma attached to unwed motherhood diminished so did the demand for the confidential confinement Marillac provided.

The 150 acres on which the original Millbury facility was located had also been purchased by Msgr. Griffin. But not for a hospital. As Brother Thomas F. Ryan, C.F.X., wrote in the 1990s in one of a series of historical articles he authored for alumni and friends of St. John High School, when Msgr. Griffin purchased the Millbury property near the turn of the 20t[h] Century he envisioned a home and school that would provide both academic and vocational courses for "poor, orphaned, neglected and delinquent boys" in the tradition of Xaverian Brothers elsewhere. The facility became a working dairy farm and cared for 30-to-40 boys at a time, but institutional commitment to the

Bishop Wright, pictured here with Father Eugene C. Archey, chaplain, and a Sister of Providence, was a frequent visitor to the pediatric ward of St. Vincent Hospital.

endeavor was lacking and after Msgr. Griffin's death in December of 1910, it faced an uncertain future. By 1915 the Brothers were forced to abandon the place that had come to be known as Mount St. Joseph Industrial School.

The fire that destroyed Mount St. Joseph Home in 1920 was not the first catastrophic blaze to afflict a Worcester County Catholic institution. Indeed, while it recovered, the survival of the industrial school that the maternity hospital succeeded was jeopardized by a fire that ravaged its principal building in 1902. Holy Cross College, too, very nearly never reopened after a blaze that began on the afternoon of July 14, 1852, destroyed much of Fenwick Hall, the building whose cornerstone was laid with such aplomb in 1843. The college did reopen, of course, a year later, but the trauma the conflagration inflicted lasted for nearly a decade. And in 1923, fire gutted the original buildings of Assumption College on Fales Street in Worcester's Greendale section. Dispiriting though that was, the college that opened in 1904 would suffer — and survive — even greater heartache in "the Tornado of 1953."

St. Augustine Church, Millville, today.

More than a dozen county churches have been destroyed by flames over the years, with several others suffering near-total losses — in the case of St. Aloysius Parish in Rochdale, two near-total losses. Parishioners of St. Luke's in Westboro, in fact, did lose two churches to fire — in 1886 and 1920 — and members of St. Joseph's in Barre nearly did. A pre-dawn blaze on May 4, 1896, destroyed the Barre Catholics' first church and also consumed the neighboring Naquag Hotel. But the church that replaced it and which still serves the town, while heavily damaged in a post-World War I blaze that spread from "Vera Wheeeeler's barn on James Street," was not beyond repair.

A suspected arsonist was arrested and charged soon after a spectacular early-morning blaze leveled St. Augustine Church in Millville on Feb. 27, 1969. But no charges were ever brought in the fire that broke out just before midnight on June 4, 1923, destroying St. Joseph Church in Charlton, even though town officials branded it as "of suspicious origin." Many believed the 19-year-old Charlton edifice was torched by the Ku Klux Klan — an opinion more widely shared the following year when a cross was burned

A spectacular early-morning fire on Feb. 27, 1969, consumed the stately St. Augustine Church, Millville. It was one of a dozen Worcester County Catholic churches totally destroyed by fire over the years. Many others, along with many Church-related institutions, have also suffered major or minor fire damage.

on the church lawn on Route 20 as plans were being completed for the construction of its replacement. During that same era, early in 1922, Northboro's Father John Sellig, who was then attending to the pastoral needs of Catholics in Shrewsbury, decided the time was right to begin celebrating Mass regularly for the Italian-Catholics who had settled in Shrewsbury's Lake Shore district. Suspiciously, a hall he had rented for that purpose burned to the ground the night before the first Mass was to be celebrated in it. Among other facilities used for Mass there until St. Anne's was dedicated on Aug. 17, 1924, as a mission of the recently-established St. Mary Parish in Shrewsbury Center, was "a worship tent" set up near the cemetery of Worcester's St. Anne Parish on the Boston Turnpike — property on which the new Shrewsbury mission church was soon built and whose name it adopted.

St. Anne Parish in Manchaug not only lost its church in an inferno that raged through that village on April 16, 1924, but also its school and the convent of the Daughters of the Holy Spirit who taught there. The homes of many of St. Anne's parishioners were also lost that day, as were mills that gave them work. St. Anne School never reopened and 29 years would pass before a replacement church was built in the village. In the meantime, as Father Richard McGrail has recorded, the parish gathered for worship "in an old community hall above a Manchaug store, the pews being a few crates and boxes."

At least two other parishes — St. Joseph's in Webster (1923) and St. Cecilia's in Leominster (1925) — lost their school buildings to flames, while an 1892 fire severely damaged the building that housed the church, school and rectory of Our Lady of the Rosary Parish, Gardner. Acts of heroism by priests, laity and firefighters,

St. Theresa of the Little Flower Church, Harvard, one of the first two parishes established by Bishop Wright, only 22 days after his installation as the diocese's founding bishop in 1950.

St. Anne Church, Manchaug, the successor to the parish's first house of worship that was lost in an inferno that ravaged the village on April 16, 1924, not only destroying the church but also the parish school and convent and the homes of many parishioners.

especially in rescuing the Blessed Sacrament and sacred vessels from burning church buildings, have been cited repeatedly over the decades, but fortunately, casualties have been few. Tragedy settled on High Street in Worcester on a bitterly cold night in January, 1892, though. Fire had already engulfed the original building of St. Gabriel Orphanage there when Father John Power, pastor of St. Paul Parish, entered it to rescue a little sick girl who had not escaped. He gathered her in his arms and fled the flames, but she died later from smoke inhalation.

Some parishioners of St. Louis Parish, Webster, maintained that their pastor, 80-year-old Msgr. James I. Mitchell, was a victim of the fire that destroyed that parish's rectory early on the Sunday morning of May 14, 1967, because four days later he was stricken ill and died. Physicians initially said the pastor's stroke could have been "remotely attributed to excitement caused by the fire" that drove him and two other parish priests from the rectory, but they later concluded it was unrelated to the blaze. Nonetheless, some townspeople would not be shaken in their belief that the revered prelate — St. Louis' pastor for a quarter-century and one of the original diocesan consultors appointed by Bishop John Wright when the Worcester diocese was founded 17 years earlier — had died "of a broken heart," certainly a fire-related trauma.

The Celtic cross in St. Anne Cemetery, Shrewsbury, marks the grave of Father John J. Power, founding pastor of St. Anne Parish, Worcester, whose burying ground it was. The present Shrewsbury church, that took its name from the cemetery whose land it shared, is in the background beyond smaller headstones that mark the graves of some of the original group of Sisters of Mercy who founded St. Elizabeth Hospital.

Unquestionably a casualty of that blaze, however, was Rev. Paul G. Dugan, St. Louis' senior curate at the time. He was forced to jump from a second-floor window when flames blocked any other means of escape. Sadly, he suffered a severely-broken right leg and head and back injuries from which he never completely recovered. He died 12 years later.

Fire, which the contemporary liturgy of the Easter Vigil employs as the pivotal symbol in representing Jesus' Resurrection — when the light of life overcame the darkness of death — played a positive role, though, in introducing the contemplative aspect of Catholic life to Worcester County residents. Members of the Order of Cistercians of the Strict Observance at the Abbey of Our Lady of the Valley in Cumberland, R.I., were anticipating a move to Spencer even before Worcester was erected as a diocese,

The "worship tent" at St. Anne's in Shrewsbury that was used during warm-weather months in 1923 and 1924 when that part of town was a mission of St. Mary Parish, but before it had its own church.

A view of the Chapter Room and retreat house from the front of the chapel at St. Joseph Abbey.

While majestic fieldstone buildings completed in later years have brought a touch 12th-Century Europe to the rolling hills of central Massachusetts, giving the area, perhaps, its most serene object of pilgrimage, the first members of what became known as St. Joseph Abbey lived in former cow barns renovated for use as cloisters, offices and sacristies. A horse barn was turned into its novitiate and a calf shed became the laundry. Fortunately, sterile rooms were available so the former dairy's bottling room became the monks' first kitchen and the pasteurizing room became the dining hall.

but Bishop O'Leary's death delayed it until approval could be obtained from his successor. Bishop Wright, therefore, set as one of his top post-installation priorities a meeting with Abbot M. Edmund Futterer, O.C.S.O., superior of the Cumberland monastery, during which the monks' plans for the 1,000-acre former dairy farm they had purchased in Spencer would be discussed. It was on March 15, 1950, that the bishop gave his approval to the proposal for the construction of a new Trappist abbey there and renovations to existing farm buildings began immediately. Six days later, however, on March 21 — two weeks to the day after Bishop Wright's installation — new urgency was given to the move when fire destroyed the monastery chapel and attached buildings at the Cumberland site.

In the (1956) book on **The Church in Worcester, New England** that he prepared with Artist Jack Frost, John Deedy, the earliest chronicler of Worcester diocesan happenings and the founding editor of *The Catholic Free Press*, portrayed the arrival of the last of the Cumberland Trappists at their pristine hilltop enclosure:

"On the day before Christmas in 1950, two ancient busses climbed snow-patched North Spencer Road and rolled to a stop outside the former hay barn of the Alta Crest Farms. Heavy bronze bells recently hung in the silo rang out a welcome as 30 hooded monks stepped from the busses and into the barn, now a chapel. There, with 60 other monks, they chanted a 'Te Deum' of thanksgiving."

A view of St. Joseph (Trappist) Abbey, Spencer.

A TIME OF "SYMPATHETIC INTEREST AND FRIENDLY FORBEARANCE"

The 1950s was a wonderful time to organize a new American diocese. The tempest-tost days of ocean crossings in the bowels of stinking ships were distant, if poignant, memories, as were the sufferings and the uncertainties brought on by the Great Depression and the horror and heartache caused by two world wars. To be sure, peace still did not reign in the world, but the pews in Catholic churches were full and with rare exception, the people were both responsive and submissive to the voice of authority. Divisive ideologies such as would be spawned later by the Second Vatican Council and the civil rights movement and the Vietnam War were, generally, non-existent in those days as, of course, were any scars inflicted by the debates over such issues as birth control and the role of women in the Church and married priests and First Communion-before-First Penance and — of all things — altar girls.

It might even be argued that an air of cockiness was about in the 1950s' Catholic community. After all, not only were its rectories and convents full, but so were its seminaries and novitiates. And Catholic people, with valued help

from the G.I. Bill of Rights that helped World War II veterans to adjust to civilian life, were entering college and the professions and buying or building homes in the suburbs in numbers hardly before imagined. Prosperity, an ironic by-product of the war-time misery that helped bridge many cultural chasms in American society, was reaching into the Catholic community.

It was into such an environment, spiced with exuberance also hardly imaginable, that Bishop John Wright entered on that late-winter day a half-century ago. Worcester, with a population of 203,486 at the time was, as now, the second largest city in New England. But in ecclesiastical circles in those days, as John Deedy observed

Bishop Wright, accompanied by Worcester Mayor Andrew B. Holmstrom, en route to a public reception in Worcester's Memorial Auditorium on the Sunday following his installation, in March, 1950.

TOP OF THE PAGE:*Bishop Flanagan bestows the abbatial blessing on Abbot M. Thomas Aquinas Keating, O.C.S.O., on Sept. 15, 1961, in St. Joseph Abbey.*

OPPOSITE PAGE: *John and Mary in the Crucifixion window in Our Lady of the Lake Church, Leominster*

laconically, "it was little more than sandwich-filling between Springfield and Boston." When the towns and cities of the county received the recognition they had long deserved, however, enormous pride overflowed. "The creation of the diocese was essentially a Catholic event, of course," said Mr. Deedy, who began reporting on its formation for the *Worcester Telegram* almost from the moment the public announcement of its creation was made at midnight on Feb. 1, 1950, "but in a wider sense it was a great community event. Worcester and the county had received a signal recognition and everyone — I can't think of an exception — rejoiced."

On any number of occasions the bishop himself recognized what he termed the "extravagant cordiality" he received from the print and electronic media, from the leaders and people of other faith communities and from public officials in the days before and after his installation. It was on one such occasion, on Jan. 16, 1952, that he may well also have fired the opening volley in the endeavor that, during the 1960s, caused George Cornell, the respected religion editor of the *Associated Press*, to dub Worcester "the ecumenical city."

Bishop Wright had been invited to speak to the Worcester Ministers' Association and used the occasion to thank the Protestant, Episcopal and Jewish clergy present for the kindnesses they and members of their

Immaculate Conception Church, Fitchburg.

St. Leo Church, Leominster.

congregations had extended to him during the previous two years. "The constant spirit among us here in the community," he said, "is one of sympathetic interest and friendly forbearance wherever interest is possible and forbearance may be needed." He acknowledged the existence in the dogmatic and spiritual realm of "fences...which it is pointless and unworthy to deny" within and between the religious congregations represented in Worcester County. At the same time, in what the *Worcester Telegram* called "an unprecedented address," he extended his pastoral hand to his audience by calling attention to "a vast field which challenges our common concern and that of our people. And in this area of social action," he said, "who would not welcome cooperation...among all men of good will, in pressing for that recognition of the sovereignty of God, the supremacy of the moral law and the primacy of the spiritual without which we can only despair of right order." In the question period that followed the talk, the bishop's implied proposal that Catholic clergy join hands with the clergy present that day in working for the common good was tentatively accepted.

Bishop Wright, who was born in Boston's Dorchester section on July 18, 1909, the eldest of six children, attended Boston public schools and Boston College and on Dec. 8, 1935, was ordained to the priesthood at the North American College, Rome. After further studies in Rome and priestly assignments in Scotland and France, Father Wright was awarded his doctoral degree in sacred theology in 1939 from the Gregorian University. For the next four years, until being named secretary to Cardinal William O'Connell, he was a professor at St. John Seminary in Brighton and on June 30, 1947 — just a few days before his 38th birthday — he was consecrated auxiliary bishop of Boston. He served Worcester County until being installed as bishop of Pittsburgh on March 18, 1959.

On April 28, 1969, Bishop Wright was given a Red Hat by Pope Paul VI and when he took up his duties as prefect of the Congregation for the Clergy in the Holy See a few weeks later, he became the first United States citizen in all Church history to assume the direction of a congregation of the Roman Curia. (Chicago's Cardinal Samuel Stritch had been named to a top curial post in 1958, but he died before taking office.) Cardinal Wright died on Aug. 10, 1979, and is buried in the Wright family plot in Hollyhood Cemetery in Brookline.

That the cardinal had an amazing intellect may never have been better ascribed than when Thomas P. McDonnell, a veteran Boston journalist, in a (1985) review of **Resonare Christum**, a three-

St. Anna Church, Leominster.

volume collection of some of the prelate's most thoughtful sermons, addresses, interviews and papers, said Worcester's first bishop may well have been "the most cultured and learned American churchman in this century....He was certainly one of the most literate of priests anywhere...." Dr. David J. O'Brien, the Loyola professor of Roman Catholic Studies at the College of the Holy Cross as the 21st Century dawned, found a hint (at least!) of such intellectual capacity in researching his President's Address to the American Catholic Historical Association in early-1999. Focusing on Bishop Wright's years of ministry in Worcester, Prof. O'Brien at one point quoted from a letter the bishop had written, following a brief vacation, to Father Daniel J. Honan, a close priest-friend in Maine. "...had a wonderful trip to Toronto," he wrote; "attended a couple of lectures on Herodotus and some of Gilson on medieval history. The best of the lectures was on John of Salisbury and the influence on him of Cicero. I greatly enjoyed it."

St. Jude Church, Rochdale, formerly a mission church and now the mother church of historic St. Aloysius-St. Jude Parish in that section of Leicester.

It is little wonder, then, that the bishop, always a public man, was in such demand to lecture, all across the country, or that national organizations readily accepted his invitations to hold meetings or conventions in his diocese. Among the most imposing and most important was the four-day National Liturgical Week held in late-August of 1955 in the Worcester Auditorium. It drew scholars and students from as far away as New Zealand — including Patriarch Maximos IV, who traveled from Lebanon on the first journey ever made to the United States by a Melkite Rite patriarch — although attendance may have been reduced somewhat when widespread flooding in preceding days caused by the torrential rains of back-to-back Hurricanes Connie and Diane made travel by air about the most efficient way to get about in central Massachusetts.

While the use of some English had been authorized that Eastertide in the administration of certain of the Church's Sacraments and blessings, Bishop Wright often quipped that it was during the Liturgical Week in Worcester in August of 1955 that the oft-maligned Catholic Vernacular Society that promoted the use of modern languages in the Mass and the Church's other liturgical rites "held its first meeting in broad daylight." Whether that was literally true matters little, because within the next decade the vernacular society's work would be vindicated throughout the Church.

Some contemporaries claimed that Bishop Wright was "hard on his priests" while he was in Worcester and saw irony in his later being named to head a Roman congregation whose principal concern is the care and well-being of the world's clergy. Other astute observers maintain, however, that despite his outreach to laity on every level — within the Church and in society — Worcester remained very much "a priests' diocese" during those years and that the bishop — who, without

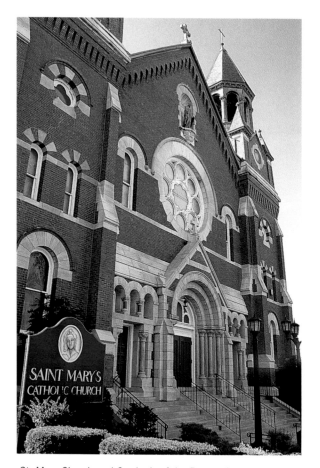

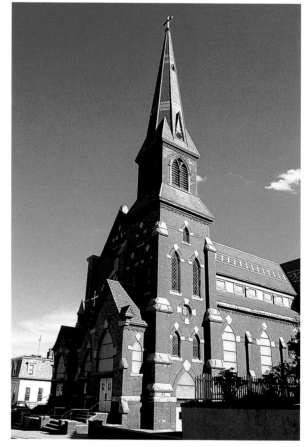

St. Mary Church and Our Lady of the Rosary Church in Spencer today serve Mary, Queen of the Rosary Parish that was established there in 1994 from the territories of two suppressed parishes that bore their names.

The entrance to the campus and Trinity Hall at Anna Maria College, Paxton. Founded in Marlboro in 1946, it moved to Paxton in 1952.

question, had late-night "telephonitis" and probably did make most of the calls to pastors in the wee-small-hours of the morning that have been attributed to him — was simply a new-style bishop for a changing Church and that he merely wanted his priests to be responsive and accountable.

It should be remembered, too, that among his first official acts relative to the clergy, was raising curates' pay by 50 percent — from $50 to $75 a month! He did not, at the same time, authorize younger priests to own automobiles — or even, as a matter of course, to hold a driver's license (after all, he didn't!). But that would come in due time — in about four years. In the meantime, the curates continued to go about their parish visitations on foot. If an emergency arose, especially at places like Worcester's City Hospital, a police cruiser would be sent to St. Paul Rectory to pick up one of the five curates then assigned there and transport him to the hospital for the "sick call."

A VIBRANT,
ENGAGING DIOCESE IS BORN

At the time of Bishop Wright's installation the diocese had 97 parishes and nine missions and, among its institutions, 46 elementary schools, 14 high schools, two colleges and three orphanages. They and the Catholic population of more than 250,000 — just about one-half of the county-wide population — were being served by an estimated 250 diocesan priests, 150 religious order priests and 1,100 Sisters and Brothers.

The bishop wasted no time in setting the foundation for what would become a vibrant, engaging diocese. At the so-called "priests' luncheon" at Holy Cross College following the liturgical rites in St. Paul Cathedral on that March day in 1950, he announced the names of the men he was inviting to share his administrative responsibilities. There were few great surprises, even though he had known few Worcester County priests at the time of his appointment. Father John F. Gannon, with whom the bishop had studied in Rome, who was the son of a public school superintendent and

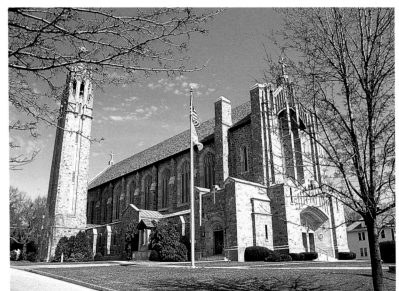

was then administrator of St. Ann (later St. Anna) Parish in Leominster, was his earliest adviser and remained as his chancellor and, later, vicar general. Father David C. Sullivan, the son of one of Worcester's first Irish-Catholic mayors, whose family owned a travel agency at "the crossroads of the county," Harrington Corner in Worcester, was recruited to give all kinds of advice on personnel and politics, ecclesial and civil, and remained as the first director of the diocesan Bureau of Catholic Charities.

Others who joined the diocesan administration included Msgr. Boleslaw A. Bojanowski (a princely Polish exile from Czarist Russia and a close friend of Pianist Ignacy Paderewski), Msgr. John P. Phelan and Fathers John J. Bell, Victor Epinard and Michael E. Lahey all named to the bishop's council for administration, and Fathers Jean B. Lamothe, James S. Barry, James I. Mitchell, John A. Martin and Michael P. Kavanagh who formed his board of consultors. Msgr. Phelan, a Worcester native who was vicar general of the former five-county diocese and administrator of both Springfield and Worcester after the Springfield diocese was divided, retained the title of vicar general until his death four days short of five years later. It was to Msgr. Phelan, then-pastor of Blessed Sacrament Parish in Worcester, Father Kavanagh, pastor of what was to become the Cathedral Parish of St. Paul, Father Epinard, pastor of Sacred Heart Parish, Southbridge, and two other diocesan consultors from the Springfield area that Bishop Wright formally presented his letters of appointment from Rome in a private ceremony in St. Paul Rectory the day before his formal installation.

The first deans of the four geographical areas of the county, outside of Worcester (the bishop was dean of the See City), were Father Epinard and Fathers Michael J. Curran, William J. Foran and Martin J. Tracy. Father John F. Reilly was

Interior and exterior views of Our Lady of the Angels Church, Worcester.

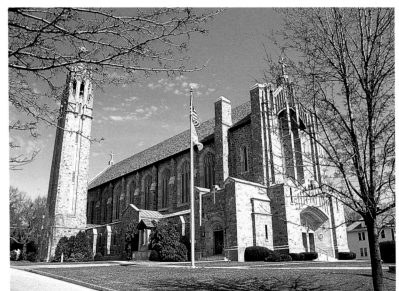

Members of the diocesan Board of Consultors scrutinized and accepted the credentials of the new bishop on the afternoon of March 6, 1950, in the cathedral rectory. Msgr. John P. Phelan, P.A., pastor of Blessed Sacrament Parish, diocesan vicar general and administrator of Springfield, and then also Worcester, since the death of Bishop Thomas M. O'Leary, second from left, was joined by Rev. Victor J. Epinard, pastor of Sacred Heart Parish, Southbridge, Rev. Michael P. Kavanagh, pastor of St. Paul Cathedral Parish, Msgr. John F. Conlin, pastor of Holy Name Parish, Chicopee, and Msgr. Thomas F. Cummings, pastor of St. Mary Parish, Northampton. Missing was Rev. E.P. Dumphy of St. Francis Parish, North Adams. The average of the five men greeting the 40-year-old bishop was 78. One of them, Father Epinard, died later that year (Oct. 20, 1950), just three days after being named a monsignor.

named chief judge (officialis) of the Diocesan Tribunal and Father John J. O'Brien was named secretary of English-language schools and Father Raymond J. Page was named secretary of French-language schools. Father Francis P. Harrity was named to head the Confraternity of Christian Doctrine and Father Joseph M. Lynch was appointed director of the Society for the Propagation of the Faith. Father Joseph P. O'Connell was selected to organize a youth guidance department to serve young people with special needs and Father Michael L. Carney was named the first secretary for Religious. Father Edward F. Kane was named chaplain of Boy Scouts and Fathers Timothy P. O'Connell and Paul F. Griffin, both of whom accompanied the bishop from Boston, were appointed secretary and notary, respectively, in the Diocesan Tribunal. Father Francis J. Manning became diocesan master of

ceremonies and Father Edmund G. Haddad was named an assistant in Chancery, working in finance. Both Fathers Manning and Haddad (who, in the diocese's early years, designed a self-insurance program that became a model for dioceses all across the land) later became chancellors of the diocese.

One of the most popular of the initial appointments was that of Father Harrity, who, as the diocese commemorated its 50th birthday on March 7, 2000, was its oldest living diocesan priest and a vibrant presence even as he approached his 92nd birthday. He had been in the vanguard of those publicly fostering Catholic intellectual pursuits prior to the diocese's establishment. In 1941 Bishop O'Leary authorized him to begin a series of monthly forums at the Bancroft Hotel in downtown Worcester that critiqued and evaluated from a Catholic perspective books then on the nation's

Sacred Heart of Jesus Church, Southbridge, which was heavily damaged in the floods that bisected Southbridge in the wake of back-to-back Hurricanes Connie and Diane in 1955. Water as deep as eight feet was measured in the body of the church.

best-seller lists. The forum, which, appropriately, was called "The Critics' Forum," brought many outstanding Catholic authorities to the city to discuss the work of contemporary authors. After 1950, with Father Harrity still in charge, the forum was renamed "The Veritas Forum" and it broadened its horizons to discuss a variety of religious and secular topics of contemporary interest. While ordinarily held in the main ballroom of "the Bancroft," and regularly attracting as many as 1,100 people, the forum occasionally ventured into the larger hall of Worcester's Memorial Auditorium where it would draw as many as 3,400 participants.

Bishop Wright had one last — nostalgic — stop to make as evening was overcoming the Holy Cross campus at the end of his triumphal installation day. After bidding his adieus at Kimball Hall to his brother-bishops and his brother-priests, the bishop, accompanied only by his driver, Leo Donnelly, and his new chancellor, Father Gannon, paid a prayerful visit to the Jesuit Cemetery near St. Joseph Chapel. There, the proper Bostonian placed a floral wreath at the monument marking the grave of Bishop Fenwick through whom the Sacraments were first brought to Worcester County.

That night, and until he purchased an episcopal residence on Worcester's west side a few weeks later, the bishop stayed in rooms provided for him by the Sisters of Providence near the maternity ward at the "old" St. Vincent Hospital. But on the morning of March 8, 1950, he used to reminisce, "the busy nine years began for serious on a gateleg table in the then-

Sisters have sideline seats at Fitton Field for the Stadium Festival in June of 1955. The event was a major annual social event and fund-raiser for the works of Catholic Charities in the diocese's earliest years.

Christina Pattee, then-12, a 7th-grader at St. Louis School in Webster, is pictured near a billboard promoting the 1973 Bishop's Fund. She submitted the motto used in the billboard that was the theme of that year's campaign. Begun in 1961 to raise funds to support charitable and educational ministries in the diocese, The Bishop's Fund-Faith in Action, as it later became known, supports some 28 diocesan ministries in whole or in part. If it reaches its Jubilee Year goal of $4.5 million it will have raised more than $87 million in support of diocesan ministries during its 40 annual campaigns.

Mercy motherhouse on High Street." That building, next to the cathedral rectory, remained the place where the direction of the diocese was mapped until a three-story residence on Tuckerman Street, near the Worcester Art Museum, was purchased about 15 months later and remodeled as the diocese's first Chancery Building.

"Busy" was certainly a word that could be used to describe those first years. But it seems hardly adequate to describe the excitement that gripped not only every parish in the county, but seemingly every Catholic household, as the bishop harnessed the lethargy of Springfield diocesan days and orchestrated a modern-day manifestation of Catholic triumphalism. Perhaps the energy the young bishop brought to the task was never more succinctly expressed than in a booklet published in conjunction with his acceptance, on April 22, 1957, of the Isaiah Thomas Award, Worcester's most prestigious civic award at the time:

Holy Family Statue at Holy Family of Nazareth Church, Leominster.

Bishop Wright celebrates a "Radio Mass" from the chapel of the Bishop's House.

'phone before others have stirred and for hours after they have called it a day."

Within days of his installation, Bishop Wright not only welcomed the Trappist monks to Worcester County, but elevated two existing mission churches — St. Theresa of the Little Flower, Harvard, and St. Anne, Shrewsbury — to parochial stature. They were the first of the 31 parishes (and five mission that would later be given parochial stature) that Bishop Wright erected during the nine years and 10 days he ministered in Worcester County in his attempt, as he told *Jubilee* magazine in 1956, to make the Catholic Church "a more indestructibly intimate part of every local community in which it finds itself."

"…here is a man who is known to travel to a distant city in the morning and be back on time to sign and post his mail in the evening; a man who of a given afternoon might deliver a paper on papal social encyclicals and that same night rally to the defense of Santa Claus in a radio commentary; a man who thrives on long hours and hard work, and who is up to answer the house

Good Shepherd Church, Linwood.

Within the five years-plus that followed (through 1955), Bishop Wright had not only founded an additional 24 parishes, but established a newspaper, an office for radio and television, and a Town and Country Apostolate aimed at keeping Catholic people in touch with their rural surroundings. He also opened the House of Our Lady of the Way that provided room, board, work and counseling services for as many as 65 homeless men at a time, established an Office for the Lay Apostolate and invited Robert H. Fouhy, a decorated veteran of the U.S. Army's 10th Mountain Division, to begin a comprehensive draft counseling service for high school youth. (It was the first of several diocesan leadership posts

The monument marking Bishop Benedict J. Fenwick's grave in the Jesuit cemetery at Holy Cross College. It was there that Bishop Wright placed a wreath of flowers at the end of his eventful installation day.

Bishop Wright and Cardinal Valerian Gracias of Bombay, India, are surrounded by teen-agers during the first county-wide convention of the Diocesan Council of Catholic Youth.

St. Boniface Church, Lunenburg.

Mr. Fouhy would hold until his sudden death in March, 1980, while conducting a seminar on the organization of diocesan deaneries at Barlin Acres, the diocese's former retreat and study center in Boylston.) During those earliest years, too, the bishop invited the Sisters of St. Anne to relocate Anna Maria College within the diocese, enthusiastically endorsed the purchase by Religious of the Cenacle of the 240-acre former Bayard Thayer Estate on Hawthorne Hill in Lancaster for conversion into a retreat house for women and welcomed several other new religious communities of men and women to Worcester County — including the Little Sisters of the Assumption who would open Pernet Family Health Service and begin nursing the sick-poor in their homes in Worcester's inner city.

Among other new religious communities was the Xaverian Sisters who opened a mission house in Petersham. They suffered a great tragedy in late-July of 1956 when two of their number, Sister Maria Grechi, S.X., and Sister Theresa Del Gaudio, S.X., en route from Italy to study American hospital techniques at St. Vincent Hospital, were lost at sea in a dense fog when the 30,000-ton "Andrea Doria" sank south of

Nantucket Island after colliding with "The Stockholm," a Swedish luxury liner. This was not the first disaster at sea to affect Worcester County Catholics. Among those lost on that fateful night in mid-April, 1912, when the "S.S. Titanic" went to the depths in the frigid waters of the North Atlantic was Father Joseph Montvila who was en route to residence in St. Casimir Parish, Worcester, whence he would minister to immigrants from Lithuania who had settled in the agricultural districts of western Worcester County in what is now St. Francis Parish, Athol. (Also aboard the "Titanic" that night was a young woman named Helen Mary Mockler from Currafarry, County Galway, Ireland, who survived the disaster and for all the years from 1916 to her death on April 1, 1984, when she was known as Sister Mary Patricia, a Sister of Mercy of Worcester, referred to herself as "a tourist attraction.")

Mother Hauley, left, and Mother Nugent, Cenacle nuns, lead retreatants in procession at the Cenacle Retreat House in Lancaster, circa late-1950s.

115

"CROWN JEWELS"
FOR A PEOPLE WITH FEW JEWELS

Interior of Holy Cross Church, East Templeton.

It was on June 1, 1951, that the Sisters of St. Anne announced the purchase of "Mooracres," a 293-acre horse farm on Sunset Lane in Paxton, and their intention to move their five-year-old women's college there from Marlboro the following summer. The manor house of the property that was converted for convent and classroom use was a then-150-year-old colonial residence that today is known as Trinity Hall on the coed campus.

Bishop Wright was not obsessed with the need for Catholic schools, especially on the elementary level. Nevertheless, during those earliest years he also encouraged the Sisters of Notre Dame de Namur to found Notre Dame Academy (for girls) at the former Ellis Estate on Salisbury Street in Worcester, invited the Brothers of the Sacred Heart to found Notre Dame High School (for boys) in Fitchburg, supported the Venerini Sisters' effort to greatly enlarge Venerini Academy in Worcester and applauded the purchase by the Sisters of the Assumption of the Blessed Virgin Mary of the 73-room former Nichawaug Inn in Petersham for transformation into a boarding academy for girls and a retreat facility for Catholic women in that part of the diocese. In mid-December, 1953, the bishop also convinced the diocesan consultors to support his decision to turn

TOP OF THE PAGE: *Mary and her Baby in Our Lady of Jasna Gora Church, Clinton.*

St. Joseph the Good Provider Church, Berlin.

116

Sanctuary of St. George Church, Worcester. The church's
stained glass windows depict only English-speaking saints.

Church of Our Lady of the Lake, Leominster.

the control of St. John High School on Temple Street
over to the Xaverian Brothers who had been teaching
there for more than a half-century. The reason, he
advised the consultors, was not only to assure high
education standards, but because "history has
proved that where a religious group actually owns a
property, they are much more zealous in taking care
of it." Further, however, the bishop saw the transfer
of ownership as part of a larger plan that would
drastically reshape the school system's secondary
school department (but which, for the most part,
was never implemented). Shortly after they
accepted ownership of St. John's High, the Brothers
purchased property in Shrewsbury and in 1961
moved the all-boys school to an extended campus
there.

Without question, the one brick-and-mortar
project that Bishop Wright esteemed above all
others was the construction of the "new" seven-
story St. Vincent Hospital atop
Worcester's Union Hill, which,
without exaggeration it might be

St. Columba Church, facing the Common in Paxton.

said, he personally supervised. The enthusiasm
that he brought to the mammoth project and the
satisfaction he experienced upon its completion
in March of 1954 are well-documented in
correspondence maintained in the diocesan
archives between him and his friend, Archbishop
Cushing. Asked, privately, at one point if in
constructing the white-and-blue St. Vincent
Hospital atop one of Worcester's highest hills he
envisioned creating a monument comparable to
the Basilica of the Sacred Heart (Sacré Coeur)
that dominates the skyline of Paris, France, the
bishop only smiled, slyly.

The affinity Bishop Wright had for the hospital
even after leaving Worcester County was
demonstrated dramatically in a telegram he sent
from Rome to *The Catholic Free Press* on June
21, 1973, only a few days after the diocesan
newspaper uncovered a plan by hospital
trustees to close its maternity section. In
initiating a debate that lasted for several weeks
(until, under public pressure, the trustees
reversed their decision), the newspaper
reported on secret negotiations the trustees had
completed and editorially chided them for
"copping out" on providing a "total family health
care practice." In his telegram to the
newspaper, published just one week after the
public furore was engaged, Cardinal Wright, who

117

Interior of Immaculate Heart of Mary Church, Winchendon

had remained a member of St. Vincent's governing board, wrote, in the truncated language of telegrams in those days, that he was "asking hospital remove my name from list lest trustees commit further indignities. Cosign my name your excellent (June 15) editorial. You speak for all friends St. Vincent on this point." While pressure was put on Bishop Flanagan (one of the two trustees to have voted against the closing, as it turned out) to have the diocesan newspaper cease and desist in its exposure of the matter, the bishop said that just, as president of the hospital corporation, he had not contravened the trustees' right to conduct their business, so, as publisher of *The Free Press*, he would not interfere with the newspaper's right to go about its business.

For all the physical development that took place during the diocese's formative years, its vitality was fed by county-wide organizations of men, women and youth that touched virtually every Catholic household. A Diocesan Council of Catholic Men would await its formal establishment until 1957, but from the moment diocesan organizational work began on the morning of March 8, 1950, a Diocesan League of Catholic Women was on the planning board. Guiding its formation was a talented young Bostonian by the name of Mildred Fleming who had come to Worcester with Bishop Wright to become, as she had been in Boston, executive secretary of the league that eventually brought together under the umbrella of the Catholic Women's Club of Worcester (of which Bishop Wright was chaplain), more than 200 parish, inter-parish and diocesan-wide women's organizations to socialize, to study, to pray and to raise funds for special projects. Involved were some 35,000 women. While the DLCW regularly sponsored courses in theology in Fitchburg and Worcester — often taught by Bishop Wright himself — the centerpiece of its annual program was a diocesan congress, held in the spring of each year in Worcester's Memorial Auditorium. The congress would probe a central theme and featured nationally-known speakers as lecturers.

Pvt. Hector Gaudette of the Massachusetts National Guard, chauffeurs Sister Elizabeth Maria, S.S.J., front, and Sister Mary Joan, S.S.J., and Sister Agnes Maria, S.S.J., on their ministrations in Southbridge following 1955 floods that devastated that part of the diocese.

OPPOSITE PAGE: *A painting of the parish's patroness in Madonna of the Holy Rosary Church, Fitchburg.*

The honorary chair of each congress was a woman who, upon recommendation of the presidents' board of the league, had been designated the diocese's "Catholic Woman of the Year" by the bishop.

Once it got going, the Council of Catholic Men was equally as efficient and effective in bringing disparate and autonomous parish and inter-parish groups together in a common diocesan-wide effort. Unfortunately, many social phenomena of the 1960s — not the least of which was the inroads television was making to reorder family life — sapped the vitality of many of those societies, although some did survive or have recently been revived.

Where there wasn't a diocesan organization to meet some group's particular needs in those days, invariably one was formed. A First Friday Club was organized early-on, for example, to encourage devotion to the Eucharist and the Sacred Heart of Jesus among business and political leaders in downtown Worcester. A diocesan-wide Guild of Catholic Nurses was formed. The Guild of Our Lady of Providence, now responding to designated diocesan needs, including the establishment of free medical clinics in local parishes, was created to assist in the work of the Sisters of Providence and the medical personnel at St. Vincent Hospital. Catholic dentists were entrusted to the care of the Guild of St. Apollonia and St. Luke Guild was organized to

Church of St. Camillus de Lellis, Fitchburg.

A 1985 sketch by Barbara Landy of St. Augustine Mission, Wheelwright. From 1895 it was a mission church of Gilbertville; it has been a mission of St. Joseph's in Barre since 1909.

encourage spirituality among Catholic physicians. The Guild of Our Lady of the Bell was organized for telephone workers and the Holy Spirit Guild — with cells in virtually every public school in the county — encouraged spirituality and social awareness among Catholic men and women teaching therein. The St. Thomas More Society was created to give Catholic jurists a common denominator and there were diocesan-wide guilds for firefighters and police officers, too. Those whom Bishop Wright called "constant greeters and ambassadors of good will" — taxi drivers — had their guild, too, dedicated to the patron saint of travelers, St. Christopher.

And while they weren't ritually organized, anglers, who — at least once a year — became consumed by the same passion as many of the Apostles, gathered together before dawn on the opening day of fishing season each year in St. Margaret Mary Church, near Worcester's Lake Quinsigamond, to call down good fortune on themselves and bad fortune on some of God's tastiest little creatures.

Equally as active — certainly more visible — during the decade or more after its organization in 1954, was the Diocese Council of Catholic Youth that brought young people together from

Windows in St. Christopher Church, Worcester

every parish and high school in the diocese to form as energized a force as ever gathered together anywhere. Geared, as were most of Bishop Wright's initiatives, to bringing people of different ethnic and social backgrounds together — perhaps for the first time — in a common endeavor, the youth council was organized, from the parish through regions of the county and onto the diocesan level like a finely-tuned political machine. Its primary goal was to encourage the nearly 15,000 young people involved, in their social and spiritual, academic and athletic development. But a major fringe benefit of the CYC effort was the camaraderie it fostered (across parish and ethnic lines) and the sense of identity it instilled in otherwise-inconspicuous young priests. (Was it a way that Bishop Wright affirmed, without confronting the tradition-bound prerogatives of older pastors head-on, the vitality and ministry of young priests who at the time — despite their many

Father James B. Kelly, one of the most active of youth council chaplains during the CYC's hay days, even sported a "CYC beanie."

years of study — had virtually no standing in the Church?)

Working under the direction of Father John P. Martin out of an impressive old home in one of Worcester's most prestigious neighborhoods that Bishop Wright had christened (Cardinal John) Newman House, the CYC's annual diocesan extravaganza was a weekend Youth Congress in the autumn of the year, complete with ball and a float-filled parade down Worcester's Main Street that regularly drew upwards of 100,000 spectators.

As part of its year-round program as many as 900 young people would often gather for dances

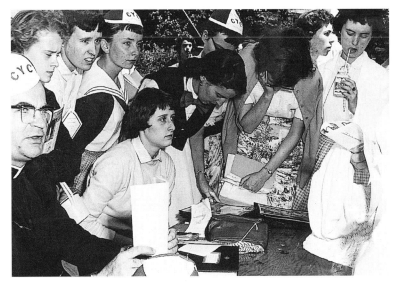

121

Bishop Wright, far left at left, leans on the stage at the end of a regular Friday Night CYC Dance at the Mount Carmel Center in Worcester and, right, leads the Rosary for shut-ins with "CYC kids" from the chapel of the Bishop's House on a Sunday evening. "The Rosary" was a nightly radio feature in those days. On Sundays it originated from the Bishop's House, on the other days of the week designated CYC groups would lead the devotion from the studios of the radio station.

on a Friday evening at Mount Carmel Center in Worcester — and invariably be joined at the end of the night by Bishop Wright, going to or from someplace. On a rotating basis, members of designated councils would also gather at a local radio station each evening (and on Sundays at the Bishop's House) to recite the Rosary over the airwaves for shut-ins. And the young people and the priest-chaplains of the nearly 145 affiliated local youth councils not only sponsored basketball and cheerleading tournaments, but debate tournaments as well. They even sponsored a giant concert band that, in 1959, appeared in concert with the U.S. Navy Band!

It's probably true, though, that the single most anticipated diocesan event in those years was the annual Stadium Festival, a variety show that began in 1952 and continued until the Bishop's Fund for Charity and Education displaced it in 1961. The Festival, coupled with an annual fund appeal in parishes, were the principal sources of income for the works of the diocesan Bureau of Catholic Charities. Staged by the staff of Catholic Charities, headed by then-Msgr. David Sullivan, with the assistance of members of the St. Vincent de Paul Society and the guilds of the Holy Family League of Charity, among others, the Festival featured many of the nation's top entertainers and invariably, as *The Catholic Free Press* once said, drew more spectators to Fitton Field than Holy Cross' football team had in years.

A window in St. Anne Church, South Ashburnham.

·GIFT OF·
Rev. J. L. Tarpy.

A FUNNEL CLOUD
DEFINES THE CHARACTER OF THE DIOCESE

A character-defining moment for the diocese came in the aftermath of a funnel cloud that formed late in the afternoon of a hot and humid June 9, 1953, in the silent surroundings of a Petersham field and began a terrifying journey through a dozen awe-struck Worcester County communities. It would leave 94 people dead, 1,310 injured (some crippled for life) and 12,000 homeless in what writer Jack Tubert later described as an "hour-long orgy of devastation." The storm was unquestionably one of the greatest meteorological catastrophes in American history. The $60 million price tag (1953 dollars) for property alone included 2,791 homes damaged and 634 homes destroyed. Also reduced to rubble was the campus of Assumption College in Greendale and among the 57 individuals killed in Worcester were two religious Sisters and one priest then living there (Sisters Marie of St. Helena, A.M., and Sister St. John of God, A.M., and Father Engelbert Devincq, A.A.).

The horror of that terrifying day was probably nowhere felt more keenly than in St. Joan of Arc Parish, Worcester, particularly in the homes of the

825 families who lived in the sprawling red brick buildings of the Curtis Apartments and Great Brook Valley Gardens, at the end of Lincoln Street. No fewer than 18 St. Joan of Arc parishioners perished in the storm and scores more were hurt and hospitalized. In all, a total of 701 St. Joan of Arc families were homeless after the vicious whirlwind jumped across Lake Quinsigamond and headed toward the tranquil neighborhoods of Shrewsbury. So heavy a human toll did the tornado exact within St. Joan of Arc's boundaries that not all of its dead could be buried from the white, colonial-style church on Lincoln Street that had been dedicated only seven months earlier.

As Bishop Wright made his rounds of the chaotic, devastated area that evening — a macabre pilgrimage that ended late into the night at the morgue of Worcester's City Hospital where,

Top of the page: "The Tornado Window" in St. Joan of Arc Church, Worcester, remembers all the dead from the 1953 storm, but especially the 18 parishioners lost to the terrible wind.

Medical personnel attend to the injured at Great Brook Valley Gardens following the 1953 tornado. Note the apartment windows; an estimated 22,000 panes of glass were broken as the twister roared through the sprawling housing development.

The battered Greendale campus of Assumption College the day after the 1953 tornado. One priest and two Sisters died there. Fortunately, all students had gone home for the summer the day before the storm struck.

simple stole draped around his neck, he anointed or blessed victims who had been taken there — he was accompanied by John Deedy who was himself reeling from the loss of all his earthly possessions that terrible Tuesday. Thankfully, the Deedy family was spared serious injury, but their home in Shrewsbury was torn asunder by the twister and its contents spread to the four winds.

If community respect for the person of the bishop — and for the Church — was not obvious by that time, confirmation came when Bishop Wright was asked to be treasurer of a three-member Disaster Relief Committee (with the editor/publisher of the local newspapers and the city manager) that was charged with gathering and dispersing relief aid to needy families. At the center of the relief effort, also, was the diocesan Bureau of Catholic Charities that put procedures into place that would be tested in times of lesser calamity later. From the moment the magnitude of the disaster became known that first evening, Father Timothy J. Harrington, then an assistant at Catholic Charities and later bishop of the diocese, established the Holy Family Thrift Shop on Green

Our Lady of the Holy Rosary Church, Clinton

Street as Ground Zero for aiding the needy and personally went to the city's radio stations to appeal to citizens outside of scourged neighborhoods to bring bedding, clothing, household appliances, foodstuffs and the like to him for immediate distribution to the needy. Thousands responded. A Catholic Charities-sponsored voucher system was also organized the following day in conjunction with a downtown department store so that disaster victims could replace essential home furnishings without charge and with as little hassle as possible.

The bountiful good will of the community that emerged from the disaster was not its only positive by-product. There was also Assumption College. The tornado might have been a death blow to that institution had not Bishop Wright — of English and Irish heritage, but a Francophile at heart — urged the Assumptionist Fathers to bequeath the little that remained of their Greendale campus to their preparatory school and to embark on an entirely new, English-speaking, college venture on property they could obtain on Worcester's "west side." Ultimately, after being itinerant scholars for three years in makeshift facilities provided by the diocese, by Holy Cross College and by Clark University, Assumption was rejuvenated in the fall of 1956 when the faculty of a budding campus on a 95-acre tract of land the Assumptionists had

The entrance to Assumption College today.

purchased on Salisbury Street welcomed its first students. Greatly enlarged, the college thrives today, like its older brother on Mount St. James and its younger sister on Sunset Lane in Paxton.

The weeks immediately following the tornado were harrowing ones for Bishop Wright. Strangely, however, they were also gratifying. As he wrote to Archbishop Cushing about five weeks after the storm: "I do find very great inspiration of a priestly kind in the sort of things I have been able to do this summer. Things that never crossed my path before."

St. Joan of Arc Parish, like Assumption College, would survive the battering it took. But it would suffer great heartache again. The parish church, which is built on land that was part of the original land grant of the King of England for what became the county seat of central Massachusetts, was named to honor the saint for whom Bishop Wright had particular affection, the youthful Maid of Orleans who was burned at the stake as a heretic after leading the Armies of France's King Charles VII to victory over English invaders in 1429. Founded on Oct. 15, 1950, it was the first parish (of seven) the bishop erected within Worcester's city limits, yet attaching Joan's name to it had more

than a sentimental connotation, since its borders embraced those sprawling public housing developments on the northeastern edge of the city that, at the time, were home to the families of hundreds of military veterans of World War II. Accordingly, when ground was broken for the church in which those families would worship, the date selected was July 4 (1951), a day that uniquely recalls the United States' own mortal struggle for independence — also from England. Just as appropriately, when the parish church to be named in honor of the solder-saint was completed, the date selected for its blessing and dedication was Nov. 11 (1952), a holiday established to remember the signing, in France in 1918, of the armistice agreements that brought World War I to an end but which was then emerging as a holiday to remember the sacrifices of veterans of all wars.

St. Joan of Arc Church that suffered two great tragedies: during the Tornado of 1953 and on Sept. 23, 1970, when Father John F. Sullivan, the parish's founding pastor, was stabbed to death by an intruder to the parish house.

Bishop Wright gave great attention to the naming of parishes he founded (and the renaming of a few others). None could have imagined, however, that the beloved pastor of St. Joan of Arc, who led that parish so tenderly in the aftermath of the "the Tornado of 1953," would suffer a death as violent as that of its patroness. But early in the morning of Sept. 23, 1970, a deranged former parishioner broke into the parish house and stabbed Father John F. Sullivan to death as he worked at the desk in his rectory study on details for the parish's 20th anniversary celebration about three weeks hence.

The death of the 67 year-old priest was a horrible parish tragedy. But the fact that Father Sullivan was also president of the diocesan Senate of Priests at the time, made it a shattering diocesan incident as well, for few priests had been involved to a greater degree in the struggle to renew the Church in the years immediately following the Second Vatican Council than he.

For the Diocese of Worcester, the break that separated the Church that emerged in the post-World War II years and that which would be fashioned during the 1960s' Council in Rome could hardly have been more clearly defined. It was, after all, on the same front page of *The Catholic Free Press* (Jan. 30, 1959) that announced Bishop Wright's transfer to the Diocese of Pittsburgh that Pope John

Our Lady of Vilna Church, Worcester.

XXIII's intention to convoke the 21st Ecumenical Council in Church history was first reported. While the idea for the Council may well have come to the Holy Father "like a flash of heavenly light," as he said later, it was received with relative calm elsewhere in the Church. Few knew what to expect. Indeed, one of the first tasks Bishop Flanagan accepted upon his installation as second bishop of the diocese on Sept. 24, 1959, was to complete the work Bishop Wright had begun in preparing for the diocese's First Synod — a gathering exclusively of priests then — that would codify for the local Church the existing general and particular laws of the Church.

Planning and convening the Synod — in St. Paul Cathedral on May 10, 1962 — was a valuable practical and spiritual exercise, of course. But the extent to which the letter — and, particularly, the spirit — of universal and, therefore, local Church law was to be influenced by the deliberations of the world's bishops at the Council that would open in Rome that autumn made many of the synod's 310 statutes (and appendices) moot almost immediately. In retrospect it can be said, however: the 1962 Diocesan Synod provides graphic insights concerning the point at which the Church in Worcester County began its journey into the era of the Second Vatican Council.

Church of St. Charles Borromeo, Worcester.

126

THE COUNCIL
AND POST-COUNCIL YEARS

When the Council Fathers had completed their deliberations and Pope Paul VI had promulgated the last of the 16 constitutions, decrees and declarations they had debated and approved and each of the 3,000-plus (arch)bishops — of every race and tongue, of every rite and circumstance of human existence — who took part in the momentous assembly had returned to his home, none became a more ardent advocate of the tenets they had collectively advanced than Bishop Bernard J. Flanagan. Many years after the Council ended he said he would "ever be grateful for the privilege of participating in the Council." It was, he said, "a spiritual and learning experience beyond any other in my life." While the memories of those four autumns in Rome — and the studying that he undertook between the annual sessions — were still vivid, Bishop Flanagan said he found it difficult "to articulate the deep-felt sense of awesome responsibility I experienced in the realization that each one of us was committed to make decisions which would affect generations yet unborn."

Bishop Flanagan — as history, even from this short vantage point, shows — not only took each vote in the aula of St. Peter's Basilica seriously, but, later, the obligation each vote imposed on him as a teacher in the Church. Indeed, he began

instructing on the "sense" of the Council and its participants almost from the moment the great gathering convened on Oct. 11, 1962, through informal but insightful "Letters from Rome" addressed to (and published in) *The Catholic Free Press.* There were 27 letters in all and while they often touched on deeply theological matters, they also brought the reader on nostalgic walks through the streets of Rome where the writer had studied for the priesthood and where he was

Top of the page: *Basilica of St. Peter, Vatican City.*

Bishop Bernard J. Flanagan

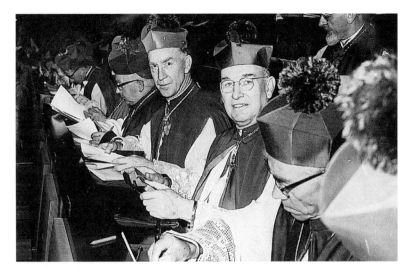

Bishop Flanagan at the Second Vatican Council. Seated on his left, here, is his North American College classmate from Raleigh, N.C., Bishop Vincent S. Waters.

being celebrated in St. Matthew Cathedral in Washington by Boston's Cardinal Richard Cushing.

Written in the gentle, tender, homely manner of a Vermont lad who, like Father James Fitton, had ministered from the Canadian border to Long Island Sound, the "Letters from Rome" belied the respected and influential position Bishop Flanagan held among his peers in the American hierarchy in those days. Bernard Joseph Flanagan, bishop, was, like most bishops of the Church, thankfully, a holy man. But he was also unpretentious, unaffected and unencumbered by the office he held. (Oh, he knew he was a bishop; he sometimes said in other contexts that it didn't matter who else knew that he was a bishop, all that mattered was that he knew!) Born in the marble town of Proctor in central Vermont, he paid his first visit to Worcester when he enrolled at Holy Cross College in 1924. Following his graduation and the completion of his priestly studies in Rome, he returned to his home Diocese of Burlington and after ministering among the Italian population of Barre for eight years got the opportunity to use his French more often when he was appointed pastor of St. Louis Parish in Highgate Center, Vt., on the Canadian border. Father Flanagan earned a doctoral degree in canon law at Catholic University in Washington before becoming chancellor of the Burlington diocese and, in 1953, the founding bishop of Norwich, a diocese bounded on the south by Long Island Sound.

ordained on Dec. 8, 1931, and even to Good Pope John's home town of Sotto il Monte in northern Italy, where the bishop made a personal pilgrimage to visit with the Pope's brother, Xaverio, and other Roncalli family members.

One letter, published on Dec. 6, 1963, told of the incredulity with which the United States bishops received the news of President John F. Kennedy's assassination and the somber and unenthusiastic manner in which they later observed their Thanksgiving Day at Rome's North American College. "This hour of national sorrow," however, Bishop Flanagan assured members of the diocese, was universally shared. To illustrate he pictured the 10,000 people — including most of the world's bishops — who crowded into the Archbasilica of St. John Lateran, Rome's cathedral, to participate in a Mass celebrated at the request of the nation's bishops for members of the diplomatic corps and American military personnel stationed in and around Rome by New York's Cardinal Francis Spellman at the very hour the Funeral Mass for the fallen President was

Bishop Flanagan's "Conciliar Ring." The simple episcopal ring was presented to each of the bishop-participants in the Council by Pope Paul VI. The inside bears the coat of arms of Pope Paul.

After returning to Worcester in 1959, Bishop Flanagan continued the physical development of the Church in the county begun by Bishop Wright. He invited the

Passionist Fathers to found Calvary Monastery in Shrewsbury, a stunning facility that would become the diocese's official retreat center, and invited members of the Order of St. Camillus to found St. Camillus Hospital in Whitinsville to serve chronically-ill and terminally-ill patients. He also brought most diocesan offices under one roof in a new Chancery Building he acquired on Elm Street and fostered the development of a counseling center for religious professionals that grew into the world's first hospice to care exclusively for troubled clergy and Religious. The House of Affirmation, as the therapeutic center headquartered in Northbridge came to be known, attracted patients from throughout the world until its dissolution in the late-1980s. The Catholic Worker Movement also took a strong foothold during Bishop Flanagan's earliest days and he developed Barlin Acres in Boylston, a 300-acre estate bequeathed to the diocese by well-known convert-philanthropists, into a study and recreation center and ultimately, after the permanent diaconate that was restored to the Church by the Fathers of the Second Vatican Council and introduced to the diocese in January of 1976, into the training center for men aspiring for ordination as deacons and their families.

St. Andrew Bobola Church, Dudley. A shrine in the building contains earth taken from several places in Poland, including the Nazi concentration camp at Auschwitz.

Interior of St. Vincent de Paul Church, Baldwinville.

It was through Bishop Flanagan's intervention, too, that St. Benedict Abbey in Still River and St. St. Mary Monastery and St. Scholastica Priory in Petersham were conceived after he and then-Archbishop Humberto S. Medeiros of Boston moved to resolve one of the unhappiest episodes in New England Church history, the post-World War II upheaval that the nation came to know as "The Boston Heresy Case." For nearly a decade after contention gripped St. Benedict Center, a gathering place for Catholic scholars and Catholic students just off Harvard Square in Cambridge, tumult surrounded Father Leonard Feeney, the charismatic former Jesuit, and the community of nearly 100 men, women and children who banded together around him and Sister Catherine Clarke as Slaves of the Immaculate Heart of Mary, an unrecognized religious community. But in 1958 they left a harried city life behind and settled in a quiet valley along the banks of the Nashua River in the Village of Still River in Worcester County's Town of Harvard. There, in buildings that date as far back as 1683, the community lived a largely-anonymous monastic life, still in isolation from the official Church, supported in great part by the farm they worked. The estrangement between the community and the Church was eased on Nov. 22, 1972, when, in a simple ceremony, "any excommunication or censures" that may have been placed against Father Feeney were lifted

Calvary Retreat Center, Shrewsbury.

through faculties granted to Bishop Flanagan by Pope Paul VI.

A little more than 15 months later, on March 4, 1974, Bishop Flanagan also accepted the profession of faith of many other members of the Still River community and absolved them "of any canonical censures which they may have incurred" for violating an interdict that had been placed on the center in Cambridge by Archbishop Cushing on Easter Monday, 1949. After Bishop Flanagan ordained Brother Gabriel Gibbs to the priesthood on Dec. 11, 1976, just three weeks after the bishop had confirmed the establishment of "The Pious Union of Benedictine Oblates of Still River" for the reconciled men and women of the center and others associated with them, a process was begun to seek formal affiliation of the men and women with the world-wide confederation of the Order of St. Benedict. Ultimately,

on Sept. 8, 1981, the first nuns of what, on Sept. 8, 1984, became St. Scholastica Priory, and the first monks of what, on March 7, 1993, became St. Benedict Abbey, recited their first, simple vows as Benedictines. Then, in the spring of 1985 the nuns of St. Scholastica Priory, under the leadership of Mother Mary Clare Vincent, O.S.B., moved to a new foundation they established on the 177-acre former "Roger Kinnicut Estate" in Petersham and soon thereafter, Father Cyril Karam, O.S.B., who was ordained a priest of the Church's Maronite Rite the day after Father Gabriel's ordination in 1976, also left Still River to found St. Mary Monastery as a companion to the Petersham priory. When the foundation in Still River was given abbatial status, Father Gabriel Gibbs, O.S.B., was elected the founding abbot.

St. Andrew the Apostle Church, Worcester.

The Church of Mary, the Mother of God at St. Scholastica Priory, Petersham.

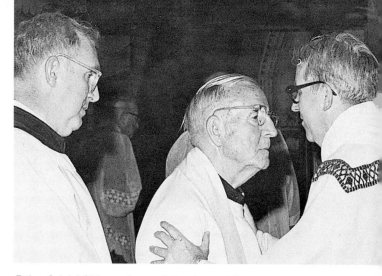

Father Gabriel Gibbs, embraces Father Leonard Feeney at the former's ordination to priesthood by Bishop Flanagan in St. John Church, Clinton, Dec. 11, 1976.

Those were not the first religious communities founded in Worcester County. In the late-1880s two young Manchaug school teachers began a trek that led to the founding of the Little Franciscans of Mary who have conducted St. Francis Home for the Aged at Thorne and Plantation Streets for more than a century, and in 1914 the Sisters of St. Joan of Arc were founded at Assumption College to provide domestic service in Catholic institutions. The young teachers from Manchaug already aspired to be Religious when the pastor of Notre Dame des Canadiens Parish recruited them to take charge of an orphanage he was establishing at a mission known as St. Anne's, in South Worcester. The women accepted the charge and, shortly, both the orphanage and the community of Third Order Franciscans they began to form had grown to the point that a second facility was opened in Auburn that they called "St. Francis Nursery." A rift developed between the women and Notre Dame's pastor, however, and all the care-givers were locked out of their quarters. In order to gain canonical recognition as a religious congregation, several of the "Sisters" went to study in a small town in Quebec and eventually took

vows as Little Franciscans of Mary. In 1897 they were received back in Worcester, but on condition that they begin ministering to the aged, leaving the care of the children at St. Anne Orphanage to Gray Nuns of Montreal who had succeeded them on Southgate Street and were by then caring for as many as 250 youngsters at a time in a more expansive facility on Granite Street. Both the ministry and the facilities of the Little Franciscan Sisters have expanded greatly in succeeding years, but changing social needs caused the closing of the Gray Nuns' orphanage in the late-1960s. When the multi-storied orphanage buildings were finally razed, five cottage-type residences were erected to accommodate needy children in more intimate family settings.

The main house (that dates from 1683) of St. Benedict (Benedictine) Abbey in Still River.

WORK TOWARD RENEWAL
GOT UNDERWAY QUICKLY

Within days of his return from Rome in 1965, Bishop Flanagan told members of the press gathered at a news conference in the Chancery Building that education would be the key to bringing the Council's work to life. The conciliar documents, he said, "have provided a challenge and all Catholics must seek ways to bring their contents, not only into their own lives but into the life of society." The manner in which the bishop faced the challenge of the

St. Francis Home, Worcester, conducted by the Little Franciscans of Mary.

St. Anne Orphanage, Worcester, that had been conducted by the Gray Nuns of Montreal.

post-Council Church may never have been better expressed than by Father John F. Burke, the chairman of the diocese's first Ecumenical Commission, founded even while the Council was still in session. "In a time when the traditional walls of the Church were tumbling down in response to the (Council's) decrees," Father Burke said, "Bishop Flanagan had the flexibility to walk over the debris and join hands in the spirit of reconstruction."

The flexibility was shown dramatically only four days after the bishop's return from the Council when he promulgated the first "Ecumenical Directory" for the diocese, setting "broad outlines" to be followed by clergy and laity in praying and working in Worcester County for Christian Unity.

TOP OF THE PAGE: *the Madonna in the House of Loreto next to Our Lady of Loreto Church, Worcester.*

One of the first of its kind in the nation, the directory was prepared by the Diocesan Ecumenical Commission that the bishop had established in May of that year, less than six months after the Council had approved its Decree on Ecumenism. In other

Our Lady of Loreto Church, Worcester.

earlier ecumenical activity, Bishop Flanagan, together with his own priests and Orthodox, Episcopal and Protestant clergy inaugurated two programs for laity that later spread to other parts of the nation: "Living Room Dialogues" and "Evenings of Christian Friendship." The bishop remained personally involved in the unity movement by co-chairing with Archbishop Iakovos, primate of the Greek Orthodox Church in the Americas, the first official discussions between Catholic and Orthodox theologians in history. They were launched at St. Spyridon Cathedral in Worcester on May 11, 1965. The bishop also encouraged the establishment of "covenants" between neighboring Catholic and Episcopal and, later, Catholic and Lutheran parishes in Worcester County. The first of those — also the first in the nation — was a covenant signed in 1970 between Notre Dame and Trinity (Episcopal) Parishes in Southbridge. Such good will grew between the priests and people of those parishes that, in 1973, in response to a statement on the Eucharist published by the Anglican-Roman Catholic International Commission, they petitioned the Pope and the Archbishop of Canterbury for permission for intercommunion. The request was turned down but, as Father Raymond J. Page and Father Edward M. Cobden, the two pastors, said

afterward in a statement applauded by Bishop Flanagan: "we submitted the request in the firm belief that Church authorities have the right and the obligation to hear the voice of the faithful."

Perhaps Bishop Flanagan's most dramatic statement in support of the Council's call for prayer and work for Christian unity came not just in the message he delivered, but in his very presence on Oct. 29, 1967, at an ecumenical service in Worcester's Memorial Auditorium arranged to commemorate the 450th anniversary of the publication of the 95 theses by Martin Luther that initiated the Protestant Reformation. Worcester's Ordinary was believed to be the only Catholic bishop in the world to take part in such a celebration. It was little wonder then, that *The Catholic Free Press* would report a few months later (Jan. 26, 1968) that the Vatican Secretariat for Promoting Christian Unity had told the co-directors of the Ecumenical Institute at Assumption College (also the first of its kind), that "the U.S. is in the forefront of the ecumenical movement and Worcester is in the forefront of most American cities."

Bishop Flanagan preaching in Worcester Memorial Auditorium at a commemoration of the 450th anniversary of the Reformation on Oct. 29, 1967.

Bishop Flanagan and Bishop Alexander D. Stewart of the (Episcopal) Diocese of Western Massachusetts entering St. Paul Cathedral.

Harrington's years as bishop, of a Commission for Women for the diocese.

Bishop Flanagan's commitment to reform was also evident in the leadership he gave to the simplification of procedures that guide Church courts, particularly marriage courts, and to his outspoken opposition to war and the armaments race, a posture that earned him association with a group of men who were both hailed and vilified during "the Vietnam era" as "peace bishops." Unquestionably Bishop Flanagan's most controversial and conspicuous ventures onto the world stage came when those matters led him to a personal meeting with Pope Paul VI in his living quarters in Vatican City and to an appearance before a committee of the United States Senate in Washington.

It was in encouraging changes in the internal structures of the Church, however, that Bishop Flanagan showed his unqualified commitment to the work of the Vatican Council. One of his first actions was to merge the Diocesan Councils of Catholic Men and Women into one body known as the Diocesan Council, which gave birth to parish councils throughout the diocese and eventually, after diocesan-wide Senates for Clergy, Religious and Laity were also established, to the formation of a Diocesan Pastoral Council that, for the most part, was elected from the grassroots on up. The effectiveness of parish councils was — and remains — spotty and the Diocesan Pastoral Council did not survive. But an idea was put forth that may well find wider acceptance in a still-evolving post-Council Church. It certainly gave inspiration to the formation during Bishop

Bishop Flanagan and Archbishop Iakovos, primate of the Greek Orthodox Church in the Americas, at Worcester's St. Spyridon Cathedral in 1965 as the historic theological dialogue they co-chaired convened.

OPPOSITE PAGE: *Window in Holy Spirit Church, Gardner.*

134

Members of the Diocesan Interim Pastoral Council at the first meeting in mid-January, 1970, are, seated from left, Jesse A. Gates, John J. Moriarty, Bishop Flanagan, council chairman, Sister Mary Cullen, S.N.D., Sister Carmen Morzillo, M.P.V., and Sister Dorothy, R.S.M.; rear, from left, are Sister Mary Behan, S.S.J., Rev. Paul M. Campbell, Dr. Vincent J. Forde, Mitchell J. Hilow, Mrs. Margaret Knowlton, Sister Mary of Providence, S.P., George J. Sonntag, Hugh J. Culverhouse, Rev. Aloysius O'Malley, C.P., Michael A. Burke and James F. Coburn Jr. Not pictured is Miss Louise Guertin. Absent were John P. Carrier, Sister Clarice Chauvin, S.S.A., Rev. Edward G. Cormier, Rev. Paul M. Couming, Brother Louis Laperle, S.C., and Rev. Thomas F. Lonergan.

Bishop Flanagan elevates the Sacred Species at the celebration of his 25th anniversary as a bishop on Oct. 9, 1978, in Worcester Memorial Auditorium. At left is Bishop Harrington, while some of the more than 250 priest-concelebrants of the Mass are pictured behind them on tiered stands set up on the auditorium's stage.

It was on Feb. 23, 1974, when "American norms" that the bishop, largely as chairman of the Canon Law Committee of the nation's bishops, had been instrumental in introducing to simplify procedures of Diocesan Tribunals were under attack in Rome, led a delegation of six American prelates (including three cardinals) to a personal meeting with the Pope.

Bishop Flanagan had the charge of presenting to the Holy Father the bishops' conviction on the "pastoral value" of the new procedures in the "administration of justice." His arguments were, obviously, persuasive because most of the norms were subsequently retained and had a positive impact on universal Church law as presented in the 1983 revisions of the Code of Canon Law.

The bishop had repeated emphatically and often the Church's teaching on peace, both as found in Scripture and as enunciated in documents of the Vatican Council. It was those beliefs, coupled with his own convictions on the current state of the world that led him, on March 1, 1972, to testify in support of amnesty for so-called "draft evaders" before a meeting of the U.S. Senate's Judiciary Committee studying military conscription.

Resurrection window in Sacred Heart of Jesus Church, Gardner.

people! — continue to perfect what was begun, the number of "firsts" rung up by the Diocese of Worcester in those first months that followed the Council Fathers' call for liturgical renewal on Dec. 4, 1963, is awesome.

"Missals" that had been carried to Mass and other devotions by people for generations so that they could follow the obscure and unintelligible actions of the priest (he was celebrating, for the most part with his back to the people and, for the most part, whispering his prayers in Latin), were suddenly obsolete, so the Diocese of Worcester organized

Nowhere was Bishop Flanagan's commitment to conciliar renewal more evident than in the leadership and support he gave to the development and implementation of a post-Tridentine (Council of Trent) liturgy for the Church. While even as the 21st Century dawns liturgists and artists, Scripture scholars and theologians, historians and musicians — and

and published its own "Mass Book" — complete with (of all things!) hymns to be sung during liturgies. (The book was later distributed nationally.) Simultaneously, the diocese was the nation's first to initiate a training program for lectors and commentators (an explanatory ministry in the earliest post-Council days) at Mass — and for priests, too.

Father Richard F. Riley, the oldest diocesan priest at the time, celebrates Mass facing the people in February of 1965 at the first permanent relocation of an altar following Vatican Council reforms. On Dec. 11, 1966, when he was pastor of Our Lady of the Rosary Church for 48 years and celebrating the 60th anniversary of his ordination, he was the only priest in either the Springfield diocese or the Worcester diocese still serving in the parish to which he was appointed by Bishop Thomas D. Beaven. Since Father Riley's arrival in Greendale, nearly a dozen parishes had been established from territory that he had served as pastor. He was fluent in both French and English.

The first Vatican Council-era concelebration of Mass in the diocese included one bishop and 12 priests. It was the Mass of the Holy Chrism on Holy Thursday, April 15, 1965. Behind them on the altar are several other priests serving as deacons of the holy oils and in pews in the body of the church are other priests. At the opening the Year of Preparation for the Holy Year on March 3, 1974, two bishops, one abbot and 96 priests concelebrated. More recently several hundred priests have concelebrated at special liturgies.

The diocese was also among the first to allow regular celebration of the Mass in the evening hours in church and at any time in homes and to anticipate celebration of the Lord's Day with Mass on Saturday evening. It was in the diocese (at St. Joseph Abbey in Spencer) where experimentation in the Rite of Concelebration of the Mass by more than one priest took place and where, at the Mass of the Holy Chrism on Holy Thursday, April 15, 1965, only two days after the initial translations and rubrics for the rite were authorized by the Holy See, that the Eucharist was concelebrated by the bishop and (appropriately) 12 priests, the number at first allowed. It was in Worcester County, too, that the first "High Mass" in English was celebrated, at St. Mary Church, Shrewsbury, on Nov. 17, 1964.

The bishop's interest in liturgy was evident from his first days in Worcester, for it was on Feb. 5, 1960, that he established the first Diocesan Liturgical Commission. With subcommittees on art and architecture and music added

later, the members issued the nation's first Diocesan Liturgical Directory on Nov. 21, 1964, the same week that authorization was received for the celebration of Mass in vernacular languages. Shortly thereafter a comprehensive directory was published on the construction of new churches or the renovation of existing churches to accommodate the demands of the renewed liturgy.

The bishop's commitment to orderly renewal was probably best stated in early-1965 when he assured pastors at a clergy conference that the liturgical renewal was not a "fad…this is the mind of the Church." And alluding to suggestions that there was a danger the renewal might result in the formation of a "high Church" and a "low Church," as happened within the Anglican Communion, the bishop said: "let me assure you, Fathers…in the Diocese of Worcester there will only be one Church."

The sanctuary of Sacred Heart of Jesus Church, Fitchburg.

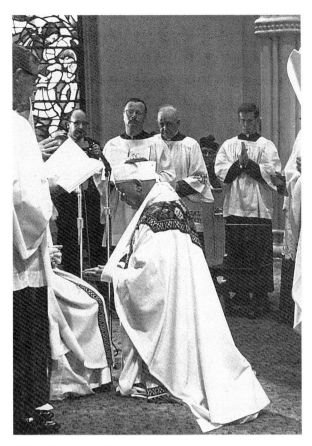

Bishop Harrington, his head and hands bound, is pictured kneeling before Bishop Flanagan at his consecration as a bishop on July 2, 1968.

The diocese, however, also saw a liturgical "last." What is believed to have been the last time the former "Rite of Consecration of a Bishop" was used in the United States was on July 2, 1968, when Bishop Harrington, until then the director of the diocesan Bureau of Catholic Charities, was consecrated the first auxiliary bishop for the diocese. Within days thereafter, the new and simplified "Rite of Ordination of a Bishop" was introduced throughout the Church.

Bishop Harrington's appointment was universally acclaimed. As Bishop Flanagan said on the morning it was announced, "I see in his appointment…by our Holy Father recognition of a record of priestly service and accomplishment which has made the new bishop one of the most beloved and highly-esteemed priests of our diocese." Similar sentiments were voiced by Cardinal Cushing who preached at the consecration ceremonies: "By his labors he has anticipated the teachings of the Second Vatican Council that we are called and privileged to be the Good Samaritan of today,

St. Hedwig Church, Southbridge.

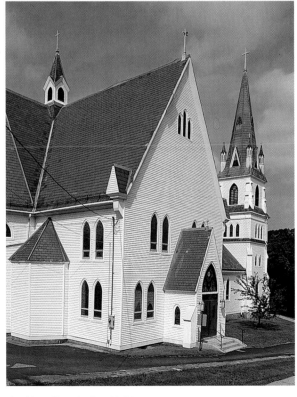

St. Mary Church, Southbridge.

helping to bind up the wounds resulting from poverty, persecution and the injustice of an affluent society where the rich become richer and the poor become poorer. By word and deed (Bishop Harrington) has charted the way of help for the poor and encouragement for the despondent. He has brought the truth of the Gospel into the field of social service and the life-giving grace of the Sacraments to those spiritually-dead from human weakness and the lack of confidence in God."

Bishop Timothy J. Harrington

The consecration of Bishop Harrington, who was dubbed by the press the "bishop of the Bowery" because of his association with the downtrodden and his residence at the time in the House of Our Lady of the Way, the diocesan hospice for homeless men, was not the first to be held in Worcester. That distinction went to Bishop Joseph N. Dinand, S.J., until then the president of Holy Cross, who, on Oct. 30, 1927, was consecrated the first vicar apostolic of Jamaica, B.W.I., in St. Joseph Chapel on the Holy Cross campus.

Born in Holyoke, one of seven children, and ordained to the priesthood on Jan. 19, 1946, following seminary studies in Montreal, two of Bishop Harrington's siblings have been among the most esteemed members of the Diocese of Springfield. His oldest brother, Msgr. John F. Harrington is a former chancellor and vicar for priests in the mother diocese and his younger sister, Sister Nora Harrington, S.S.J., is a former chemistry professor and long-time vice-president of The Elms College. Ties to the past were evident at the bishop's consecration in 1968. While Bishop Flanagan was the consecrating prelate, the co-consecrators were Bishop Wright, then in Pittsburgh, and Bishop Christopher J. Weldon, who assumed leadership of the Church in the four western counties of the commonwealth at the time of the division of the old diocese in 1950.

Perhaps the diocese never experienced a more exuberant moment than that on the evening of Oct. 13, 1983, when a beaming Bishop Harrington rose from his chair on the stage of Worcester's Memorial Auditorium, just after being installed as successor to Bishop Flanagan as head of the diocese, and, arms outstretched, his crozier in his left hand, said simply: "Wow!"

Bishop Harrington and Bishop Robert Isaksen, head of the New England Synod of the Evangelical Lutheran Church in America, right, are pictured in Blessed Sacrament Church, Worcester, on Jan. 20, 1991, as they signed an historic covenant agreement making more "solemn" the relationship between the Diocese of Worcester and the Lutheran synod. That relationshhip made another historic advance on June 1, 2000, when Bishop Reilly preached at the Eucharistic service opening a synodal assembly in Sturbridge convened to elect a successor to Bishop Isaksen. It was said to have been the first time a Catholic bishop had preached in such a setting.

Throughout his 11 years as Ordinary of the diocese, Bishop Harrington remained an active participant in the work of the national office of Catholic Charities and of Catholic Relief Services, the U.S. bishops' overseas relief arm. He took particular pride in introducing to the diocese the Rite of Christian Initiation of Adults which restored many former practices to the ritual of welcoming adults to the worship life of the Church.

Sadness gripped the diocese over a 10-month period in 1997 and 1998. It was on March 23, 1997, that Bishop Harrington succumbed, at age 78, and it was on Jan. 28, 1998, that Bishop Flanagan died, just two months before his 90th birthday. Both men had submitted their resignations, according to post-Vatican Council Church custom, upon reaching their 75th birthdays. Each rests today in the "priests' plot" in St. John Cemetery.

Bishops Harrington and Dinand are among the more than 40 men who were born in Worcester County or who served in its parishes or were associated with its educational institutions who, over the years, have been raised to the Catholic hierarchy. They include not only Bishop James A. Healy, the nation's first bishop of African-American ancestry, but also Bishop Donald E. Pelotte, S.S.S., of Gallup (N.M.), the nation's first bishop of Native American ancestry, who began his priestly studies in Barre when the Blessed Sacrament Fathers had their novitiate there (1946-1976). They also include men like Fathers Philip J. Garrigan and Thomas J. Conaty, both former curates at St. John's in Worcester and later pastors, respectively, of St. Bernard's in Fitchburg and Sacred Heart Parish, Worcester, who, as (first) vice-rector and (second) rector of The Catholic University of America around the turn of the 20th Century, may well have been the stabilizing influences that saved that institution from collapse after the highly-esteemed founding rector, Bishop John J. Keane, formerly of

Bishop Thomas M. O'Leary of Springfield, left, poses outside St. Joseph Chapel at Holy Cross on Oct. 30, 1927, after consecrating Bishop Joseph N. Dinand, S.J., the college president, right, to be vicar apostolic of Jamaica, B.W.I.

Richmond (Va.), was called to Rome to answer unflattering ("Americanist") charges leveled against him by powerful prelates. The two Worcester County priests later went on to become bishops, respectively, of Sioux City (Iowa) and Monterey and Los Angeles (Calif.).

The list of episcopal appointees with Worcester County connections also includes Bishop John A. Marshall, a native of Worcester's St. Paul Parish, who was business manager of Rome's North American College when he was named bishop of Burlington (Vt.) in late-1971. While Bishop Harrington, who also was a Holy Cross College alumnus, was a priest of the Diocese of Worcester at the time of his elevation to the

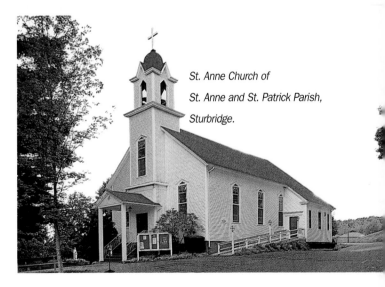

St. Anne Church of St. Anne and St. Patrick Parish, Sturbridge.

Bishop John A. Marshall, a former Worcester diocesan priest, lays his hands on Bishop George E. Rueger during the ceremony at which Bishop Rueger was ordained a bishop on Feb. 25, 1987, in St. Paul Cathedral.

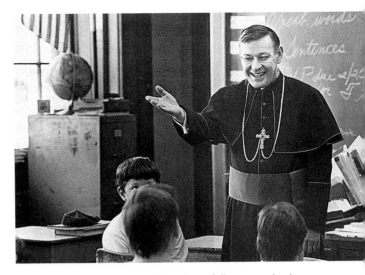

Bishop Rueger, a former superintendent of diocesan schools and long-time vicar for education in the diocese, visits with students in what was then known as Worcester Central Catholic Elementary School.

hierarchy, he was originally ordained for the Diocese of Springfield — thus, Bishop Marshall, who, at the time of his death in 1994 was bishop of Springfield, has the distinction of being the first priest ordained specifically for the Worcester diocese to become a bishop. The second priest so ordained was Auxiliary Bishop George E. Rueger, who grew up in St. Peter's in Worcester, went to Holy Cross and St. John Seminary, Brighton, and was pastor of the parish of his youth when he was ordained a bishop on Feb. 25, 1987. A former superintendent of diocesan schools, Bishop Rueger is now the vicar for education and vicar general of the diocese.

Bishop George E. Rueger

Then-Father John Marshall is not the only priest to have held high office beyond the diocese's boundaries. Father John D. Thomas, at one time the diocesan superintendent of schools, is also a former business manager of the North American College and Father John Bagley, later chancellor of the diocese, was assistant superior of the North American College's Graduate House of Studies during a period when he was director of the American bishops' Office for U.S. Visitors to the Vatican. Msgr. John F. Gannon and Father Henry G. Bowen were presidents of the Canon Law Society of America, and Father Paul T. O'Connell was its secretary for several years. Msgr. Anthony S. Czarnecki is a former director of the American bishops' office for ministry to refugees and Father James P. Moroney presently heads the bishops' liturgy office in Washington. Msgr. Francis D. Kelly, former head of the religious education department of the National Catholic Educational Assn., is presently rector of Pope John XXIII National Seminary for delayed vocations in Weston and Father James A. Houston was international director of the Emmaus Spirituality Program for Priests for many years. Msgr. Michael W. Banach, a member of the Vatican Diplomatic Service, is presently assigned to the Office of the Secretary of State in Vatican City.

Laity from the diocese, too, have held high office in Church organizations over the years. Not only was Dr. David O'Brien president of the American Catholic Historical Association, but Luke H. Richard Jr., former cathedral organist and choir director, was president of the National Association of Cathedral Organists and Choirmasters. Joseph J. Maguire, a Worcester native and Holy Cross College dean, and Dr. John K. Zawacki of Northboro, a physician on the staff of UMass Medical Center, have both been president of the National Advisory Council of the U.S. bishops' conferences

And, while they were never officially members of the diplomatic corps, several Assumptionist priests closely associated with Assumption College, were chaplains to the American diplomatic colony in Moscow — and the only Catholic priests tolerated in the Soviet Union — throughout the years of World War II and the Cold War. Their presence was guaranteed by the 1933 agreements that established diplomatic relations between the U.S. and the Soviets. The first of their

Bishop Flanagan chats during the Second Vatican Council in Rome with Catherine (Kennedy) McCarthy, a former Worcester school teacher, who was a lay auditor of the Council.

number, Father Leopold Braun, A.A., served from 1933 to the war's end in 1945, although most headlines connected with their service were reserved for Father Georges Bissonnette, A.A., and Father Louis Dion, A.A., who were caught in the web of Soviet intrigue at the height of the Cold War.

Nor should it be forgotten that two religious order priests from Worcester County, Father Killian Healy, O. Carm., a native of Worcester, and Father Wilfrid J. Dufault, A.A., a former Assumption College president and native of Spencer, were also Fathers of the Second Vatican Council as the major superiors, respectively, of the Carmelites and the Augustinians of the Assumption. Each was the first American to hold the top leadership post in his world-wide congregation. Another Council participant was Catherine (Kennedy) McCarthy, a former Worcester school teacher who, while residing in San Franciso, was elected president of the National Council of Catholic Women and was one of the first lay auditors of the Council appointed by Pope Paul VI.

St. Mary of the Hills Church, Boylston.

A TIME FOR HEALING
AND NEW BEGINNINGS

Just as then-Father Fenwick was sent to Charleston in 1818 to heal the wounds that had torn the Church in that seaport city asunder, and just as Father Fitton was sent to Providence in 1843 to resolve the dispute that threatened irreparable harm to the infant Church there, so did Bishop Daniel P. Reilly accept his call, in late-1994, to become the fourth bishop of Worcester in New England.

Over the years there, of course, had been other disputes within the central Massachusetts Catholic community — some far more devastating than that which came to be known as "L'affaire St. Joseph." There was, for example, the episode in North Brookfield in the late-1890s when residents of "Little Canada" who, at the time, comprised about one-third of the population of St. Joseph Parish there, became incensed at what they believed was Bishop Beaven's insensitivity to their requests for "a priest of our own" and, after an appeal to Rome failed, formed L'Association religieuse Canadienne-Française, built a chapel and brought in a French priest (Jean Berger) to minister to them in French. In 1900, as Dr. Claire Quintal, director of the French Institute located on the campus of Assumption College, explains in *Steeples and*

Smokestacks, a (1996) collection of essays that she edited on the Franco-American experience in New England, the "dissidents" were subsequently excommunicated, the chapel was padlocked, litigation was undertaken and threats were made to establish a French-language Protestant church. However, Prof. Quintal observed, "no resolution of the conflict was ever reached."

There were situations in Webster and Worcester, too, soon after the turn of the 20th Century, when Polish immigrants became so upset with the pastor of St. Joseph Parish that they left to found Webster's Polish National Church and when Lithuanians, disenchanted with the pastor of St. Casimir Parish, broke away and organized a Lithuanian National Church in Worcester's Island District off Millbury Street.

And there was the infamous "Palm Sunday Riot" of 1847 in Worcester when frustrated and disconcerted Irish workers besieged St. John Rectory and

A window depicting the parish's patron in St. Pius X Church, Leicester.

TOP OF THE PAGE: *a grouping of Our Lady of Fatima on the grounds of Our Lady of Mount Carmel Church, Worcester. In the rear are the "Mount Carmel Apartments," the only parish-sponsored housing complex in the diocese.*

St. Joseph Church, Leicester.

confronted Father Matthew Gibson, whom they contemptuously called "the landlord's priest," physically dragging him from the rectory and forcing him to flee the city — for his life, he believed — on the night train to Boston.

Nor, in more recent memory, was the appeal of parishioners of St. Joseph's in Worcester to the apostolic pro-nuncio in Washington for relief from what they believed was episcopal misfeasance, unprecedented. Members of St. Anthony of Padua Parish, then in Webster, also took such action in their rebellion against Bishop Flanagan's decision in the late-1960s to

build a new St. Anthony Church in Dudley that would serve not only all Slovak peoples in the area, as the Webster church had for some 50 years, but also all non-Polish-speaking Catholics in that adjoining town. A "Committee to Save St. Anthony's" did not prevail, but a vibrant nationality-territorial parish resulted.

All those things happened, though, in the days before satellite dishes and around-the-clock radio and television newscasts.

When Bishop Reilly was installed as Ordinary on Dec. 8, 1994, the diocesan family was still suffering the aftereffects of a controversy that erupted in early-February, 1992, when Bishop Harrington announced plans to close St. Joseph Church on Worcester's "French Hill" and to merge the parish it served with that from which it had been separated a century earlier, Notre Dame des Canadiens. The dispute that flowed from those decisions was bathed in the world's media spotlight for the many months that it made its way through both Church and civil courts. Without question the darkest day in the drama was June 23, 1993, when Worcester police unenthusiastically enforced an eviction order obtained by Bishop Harrington in Massachusetts' Superior Court and escorted from the church the last 49 members of a group who had taken control of the edifice just prior to its scheduled closing — and occupied it for 13 months. Armed during their ceremonious exodus with Rosaries and Crucifixes, prayer books and candles, the 49 dissenters were the rear guard of a cadre of some 250 men, women and young people who, throughout the long siege, had held prayer

St. Anthony of Padua Church, Dudley.

145

Interior and exterior views of St. Joseph Church, Worcester.

services in the church by day and by night. The occupation was widely acknowledged as the longest such demonstration in American Catholic Church history.

Bishop Harrington said he had come to his "most difficult" decision to close the church because it needed extensive — and expensive — repairs and because a diminishing number of priests in the Worcester diocese necessitated consolidation of parishes. Bewildered parishioners said their decision to occupy the church grew from a conviction that insufficient consultation had been held before the decision was made to close it. Ronald B. Fortin, a parishioner for about six decades at the time, the brother of two priests and chairperson of the "Committee to Save St. Joseph's" that was the people's nerve center in the confrontation, said the issue was not whether the then-65 year-old parish church that fine arts experts had described as a "magnificent blend of Gothic, Byzantine, Romanesque and Renaissance architectural styles" should be preserved, but "whether a community of faith, a vibrant and prayerful community that has always paid its bills should survive."

From the time of his arrival in Worcester Bishop Reilly made no secret of his desire to seek healing and reconciliation between the diocesan

St. Denis Church, Ashburnham, the second oldest church edifice in the diocese. A former Methodist church, built in 1832 it was purchased by Ashburnham Catholics in 1871 and dedicated to St. Dennis (sic) by Bishop Patrick T. O'Reilly on Oct. 26, 1873.

St. Joseph Church, Auburn.

administration and the people who, in the wake of the eviction that was carried to television screens around the world, continued to pray daily on the Hamilton Street sidewalk in front of their boarded-up and fenced-in church. A Reconciliation Committee Bishop Reilly soon appointed did not revisit Bishop Harrington's decision to merge St. Joseph and Notre Dame des Canadiens Parishes, but it did review all issues surrounding the closure and occupation of the church. Ultimately it recommended that the decision to close be rescinded.

The enthusiasm with which Bishop Reilly received the committee's recommendation was apparent at a Mass he celebrated in an unpadlocked St. Joseph Church on the afternoon of Aug. 4, 1995. Standing in a sanctuary banked with summer flowers and flanked, significantly, by 12 concelebrating priests, a beaming bishop looked across the faces of some 1,000 worshipers gathered in the resplendent structure and said simply: "My dear friends. Welcome home." Because of the thunderous applause that

Bishop Daniel P. Reilly

resounded through the vaulted church, many in the congregation did not hear the bishop repeat his greeting — in French. Everyone heard however, when he stretched out his arms and proclaimed: "hardened hearts have softened...your prayers have been answered...reconciliation is at hand...St. Joseph's Church is open and alive again!"

That was not the first time an incumbent Worcester diocesan bishop had set aside a decision of a predecessor. Soon after his appointment in 1959, Bishop Flanagan revised part of a plan initiated by Bishop Wright in early-1956 to suppress St. Joseph Parish in Leicester and to establish from its territory two new parishes, St. Pius X in Leicester Center and Our Lady of the Valley in the Cherry Valley section of town. The plan also called for the razing of the then-90 year-old St Joseph Church and replacing it with a new Our Lady of the Valley Church farther east on Route 9. While a new St. Pius X Church was completed before Bishop Flanagan's installation, afterward he decided to scrap plans for Our Lady of the Valley Church and, instead, to complete necessary repairs on St. Joseph's and to restore its name and its dignity as the town's mother church.

Also upon his arrival in

central Massachusetts, Bishop Reilly said he was not in the business of closing churches or schools or any other institution. As if to bring theological authority to his conviction, he asked the congregation at the Aug. 4 Mass in the reopened St. Joseph's in Worcester to ponder "how fortunate we are to believe in God; how fortunate we are to believe in God's love for us…how fortunate we are to believe that we are also God's people." And, he added, "it is because we are a people of faith and because we are God's people that we have this beautiful house that is God's house, the house of God's people."

"I know you know that," the bishop continued, gesturing toward the congregation. "That's what motivated you" over the last four years. "You've worked so hard….It makes me happy to see people loving their church. We need more people loving their church." Then, paying the beleaguered community the ultimate compliment, Bishop Reilly said "St. Joseph Church should be for us in the Diocese of Worcester, a sterling example of faith in action." It should be, he continued, "an example of determination in distress, of trust in the midst of doubt and of reconciliation in love." In the future, Bishop Reilly said, his voice dropping almost to a whisper, "I don't want people to point to St. Joseph's and say 'that was the church that was closed and is now reopened.' I want them to point to this beautiful church and say 'what a people they are! They have such faith! They do such great things!'"

The words were a challenging echo of others spoken two generations earlier in tribute to the

St. Thomas Aquinas Church, West Warren.

even earlier generations who had built St. Joseph's and scores of other churches and Catholic institutions in Worcester County in the years before the establishment of the New World's Diocese of Worcester. In his installation homily during that memorable Mass on March 7, 1950, Archbishop Cushing said:

"No one can read without tears of gratitude of the great (priests and laity and consecrated Religious) whose spiritual and bodily strength brought the faith to Worcester County in years gone by. 'Erant gigantes in diebus illis!' 'There were giants in those days!' We read of the incredible sacrifices with which our sometimes-unwelcome Catholic ancestors, with personal labor — after a hard day's work was over — footed the weary shovel with their sturdy feet and softened the reluctant soil of Worcester (County) hills. We should neither forget nor be ashamed to proclaim that our foundations here were dug with the same honorable picks with which our ancestors also earned their subsistence in days less propitious for our people than today. Thus, baptized with noble sweat, were laid the foundations of each House of God hereabouts."

"Dear members of the Diocese of Worcester that is born today," Archbishop Cushing advised in that homily at Bishop Wright's Mass of Installation, "be worthy of those who have gone before you in the Sign of Faith and sleep the sleep of peace!"

St. Joseph Church, Gardner.

A GIANT ACHIEVEMENT
FOR A NEW MILLENNIUM

It was the challenge of such a sentiment that, without doubt, caused Bishop Reilly, as the Third Millennium of Christianity was dawning a half-century later, to initiate a gigantic effort that would help preserve what earlier generations had built and bequeathed.

Soon after he was installed late in 1994, the man who would start singing "Danny Boy" at the drop of almost anyone's hat, said he wanted to be a cheerleader-of-sorts for the priests and deacons, the Sisters and Brothers, the lay men and women and, especially, the young people ministering in the marketplace of Worcester County or within its 126 Latin Rite parishes and two missions, its two Eastern Rite parishes and in diocesan and allied agencies and institutions. Bishop Reilly knew something of being a cheerleader, he had said,

having been born into a family of nine siblings in Providence. He also knew something of being an administrator, having been chancellor and vicar general of the Diocese of Providence before being appointed bishop of Norwich in 1975, the office he held when he was appointed bishop of Worcester by Pope John Paul II. That Bishop Reilly should have sought to restore serenity to "French Hill" was no surprise to anyone who understood whence he came. After all, he was ordained to priesthood (in Providence on May 30, 1953) following five years of study at the Seminary in St. Brieuc, France, and was ordained a bishop on the

Bishop Reilly signs parchments designating the churches of 10 diocesan parishes as Jubilee Churches for the celebration of the Millennium in the Year 2000. The celebrations included pilgrimages from throughout the diocese to those churches as well as Holy Year/Golden Jubilee journeys by nearly 250 diocesan pilgrims through the Holy Land, France and Germany, culminating in a June visit to Rome and Mass with the Holy Father at the conclusion of the International Eucharistic Congress. Later in the year the bishop planned to visit Worcester, England, and to lead groups of pilgrims to Worcester County's ancestral cathedrals in Baltimore, Boston and Springfield.

St. Peter Church, Petersham.

Feast of the Transfiguration (Aug. 6) in 1975. Perhaps more relevant, however, was that among the responsibilities he had accepted as a member of the post-Council National Conference of Catholic Bishops was the co-authorship (with a small group of bishops chaired by Cardinal Joseph Bernardin of Chicago) of the momentous pastoral letter advocating peace throughout the world that the nation's hierarchy overwhelmingly endorsed (238-9) in 1983.

Along with restoring harmony on Hamilton Street, Bishop Reilly, early-on, confronted two areas of Church life in Worcester County that had recently been afflicted with fits of pessimism: priestly vocations and Catholic schools. As part of his effort to reenergize a vocations recruitment program, he opened "Father Fitton House," a modern adaptation of the minor seminary tradition that introduced earlier generations of young men to the priesthood. Named, appropriately, after Worcester County's first resident priest, Fitton House is a place where aspirants can live and pray and assess while pursuing undergraduate degrees in local colleges and universities.

Also within months of his installation Bishop Reilly had not only approved plans for the opening of the first parish school in the diocese in nearly 30 years — in St. Bernadette Parish in Northboro — but had authorized the reinstatement or the addition of new grades to several other parish and diocesan schools.

As the Jubilee Year for the Universal Church and the diocese approached, Bishop Reilly also initiated a program to endow, "well into the future," diocesan parishes and schools and vocations recruitment, social

St. Mark Church, Sutton.

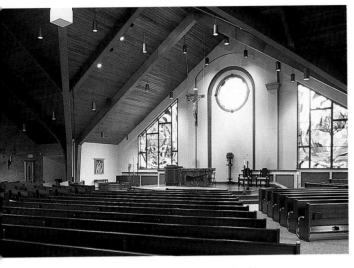

Interior of St. Rose of Lima Church, Northboro.

St. Bernadette Church, Northboro.

service and religious education programs and health and retirement programs for priests. Called "Forward in Faith," it was a $40-million capital fund campaign — that was oversubscribed by more than 25 percent. In assessing final donations in excess of $51.8 million to the year-long effort early in 2000, Bishop Reilly said, "this campaign must be considered one of the most significant accomplishments in the history of the diocese." Fund raisers called the results "unprecedented," claiming that the amount exceeded the yearly Offertory income in diocesan parishes by 216 percent. "This is a benchmark for other dioceses," the fund raisers maintained.

Of the amount raised, some $32,000,000 was earmarked for defined diocesan endowments and, in accordance with a sharing agreement built into the fund effort, some $19,000,000 was to be assigned to the parishes for their use in improving facilities and programs and, as the bishop said, to provide "for the training and sustaining of new parish ministers."

Bishop Reilly said that while diocesan fiscal leaders had advised him that "an infusion of financial resources was necessary to sustain as well as to develop the mission of our local Church," he had undertaken the "Forward in

Faith" effort reluctantly. But he finally did so "buoyed," he said, "by a history of extraordinary faith, continuing generosity and exemplary dedication on the part of the priests and people of the diocese." The final result, the bishop observed, "represents the marvelous coming together of the best in our diocese for a challenging and worthy cause...we can all be proud of what we have accomplished for our beloved Church and its on-going mission."

If Bishop Reilly's concurrent prediction is correct that "this achievement and all who made it possible will be long remembered and praised in our diocese," the stature ascribed by Archbishop Cushing to the immigrant settlers who dug the foundations for the Church in Worcester County might well also be applied in the future to their grandchildren and great grandchildren and great great grandchildren who endowed the fruits of their forebears' labor with Year 2000 gifts.

St. Mary Church, Shrewsbury.

CHRONOLOGICAL LISTING
OF ALL CATHOLIC PARISHES
IN WORCESTER COUNTY

With the founding date (as parish) and the name of the founding
pastor/first resident priest of each

PARISH	CITY/TOWN	ESTABLISHED
St. John the Evangelist Rev. James Fitton	Worcester	05/ /1836
St. Mary of the Assumption Rev. George A. Hamilton	Milford	02/04/1850
St. Paul the Apostle Rev. Charles O'Reilly	Blackstone	11/23/1850
St. Brigid Rev. Zéphyrin Lévesque; Rev. Michael J. Dougherty	Millbury [9, 12]	10/01/1851; 06/30/1869
St. Louis Rev. J. E. Napoléon Mignault	Webster	11/30/1852
St. Mary of the Assumption Rev. Edward J. Sheridan; Rev. Denis A. O'Keefe	Uxbridge [9]	08/ /1853; 05/ /1867
St. Bernard Rev. Edward Turpin	Fitchburg	01/ /1856
St. Anne Rev. John J. Power	Worcester [2]	08/06/1856
St. John the Evangelist Rev. John J. Connolly	Clinton	12/01/1862
St. Martin Rev. Thomas H. Bannon	Templeton/Otter River	01/ /1864
St. Mary of the Angels Rev. Angelus M. Baret	Southbridge	09/11/1865
St. Joseph Rev. Edward Turpin	North Brookfield	07/20/1867
St. Paul (Cathedral) Rev. John J. Power	Worcester [10]	07/04/1869
Notre Dame des Canadiens Rev. Jean Baptiste Primeau	Worcester [3]	09/10/1869
Notre Dame Rev. Michel F. LeBreton	Southbridge	11/29/1869
St. Philip Benizi Rev. Angelus M. Baret	Grafton	11/ /1869
Our Lady of Good Counsel Rev. Anthony J. Derbuel; Rev. William F. Smith	West Boylston [9]	/ /1869; 07/15/1928
Sacred Heart of Jesus Rev. Jules Cosson, O.M.I.	Webster	01/ /1870
St. Denis Rev. Louis G. Gagnier	(East) Douglas	10/26/1870
St. Luke the Evangelist Rev. Richard J. Donovan	Westboro	11/06/1870
Immaculate Heart of Mary Rev. Denis C. Moran	Winchendon	07/31/1871
Our Lady of the Rosary Rev. Jules Cosson, O.M.I.	Spencer [4]	01/ /1872-12/31/1993

OPPOSITE PAGE: *A portrayal of the parish's patron in Sacred Heart of Jesus Church, Milford.*

PARISH	CITY/TOWN	ESTABLISHED
St. Paul Rev. A. Romano	Warren	12/ /1872
St. Leo Rev. Daniel Shiel	Leominster	01/02/1873
Immaculate Conception Rev. Robert Walsh	Worcester	11/07/1873
Sacred Heart of Jesus Rev. James T. Canavan	Fitchburg	01/09/1880
Sacred Heart of Jesus Rev. Thomas J. Conaty	Worcester	01/24/1880
Sacred Heart of Jesus Rev. Michael J. Murphy	Gardner	02/ /1880
St. Joseph Rev. David F. McGrath	Leicester	08/01/1880
Our Lady Immaculate Rev. Edward F. Martin	Athol	03/10/1882
Our Lady of the Assumption Rev. Joseph A. Charland	Millbury	04/20/1884
St. Peter Rev. Daniel H. O'Neill	Worcester	05/15/1884
St. Augustine Rev. Michael H. Kittredge	Millville	10/14/1884
Our Lady of the Holy Rosary Rev. Isaie Soly	Gardner	11/ /1884
St. Mary Rev. James F. McCloskey	Holden/Jefferson	/ /1884
St. Mary Rev. Cornelius J. Foley	Brookfield	05/ /1885
St. Roch Rev. Charles J. Boylan	Oxford	05/ /1886
Immaculate Conception Rev. Clovis Beaudoin	Fitchburg	10/05/1886
St. Matthew Rev. John F. Redican; Rev. John J. Bakanas (resident administrator)	Southboro/Cordaville [9]	11/03/1886; 08/18/1956
St. Mary Rev. Charles R. Viens	Spencer [4]	12/16/1886-12/31/1993
St. Rose of Lima Rev. James F. McCloskey	Northboro	/ /1886
St. Stephen Rev. Richard S. J. Burke	Worcester	01/27/1887
St. James Rev. Michael J. Carroll	(South) Grafton/Fisherville	02/07/1887
St. Anne and St. Patrick Rev. Jules Graton	Sturbridge/Fiskdale [7]	/ /1887
St. Joseph (Basilica) Rev. Francis S. Chalupka	Webster [11]	05/21/1888
St. Patrick Rev. Peter S. O'Reilly	Northbridge/Whitinsville	05/ /1889
St. Joseph Rev. Joseph A. Forest	Fitchburg	07/06/1890
St. Joseph Rev. Jules Graton	Worcester [3]	03/09/1891
Holy Name of Jesus Rev. Joseph-Edmond Perreault	Worcester	02/08/1893
St. Thomas Aquinas Rev. Humphrey J. Wren	West Warren	12/ /1893
St. Aloysius Gonzaga Rev. William F. Grace	Hardwick/Gilbertville	02/25/1894
St. Casimir Rev. Joseph Jakstys	Worcester	10/21/1894

Our Lady in St. Cecilia Church, Leominster

PARISH	CITY/TOWN	ESTABLISHED
St. Anne Rev. David Moyes	(South) Ashburnham	08/23/1895
St. Augustine Mission At first a mission of Gilbertville, since 1909 a mission of Barre	Hardwick/Wheelwright	07/07/1895
St. Anne Rev. William Finneran	Southboro [9]	/ /1899
St. Cecilia Rev. Wilfrid Balthasard	Leominster	01/07/1900
St. Anne Rev. J. Victor Campeau	Sutton/Manchaug	01/21/1900
St. Joseph Rev. John J. Bell	Charlton City	03/25/1900
Holy Angels Rev. Richard J. Burke	Upton	12/14/1900
Our Lady of Czestochowa Rev. Jan Z. Moneta	Worcester [12]	09/01/1903
St. Francis of Assisi Rev. Louis-Alfred Langlois	Fitchburg	09/17/1903
St. Joseph the Carpenter Rev. Michael W. Mulhane	Barre	11/02/1903
St. Peter Rev. Joseph J. Rice	Northbridge	01/01/1904
St. Anne Mission It had been a mission of Our Lady Immaculate, Athol, and St. Peter, Petersham	(North) Dana [1]	01/ /1904-04/27/1938
St. Anthony Rev. Joseph E. Chicoine	Worcester [6]	06/01/1904-12/31/1975
Good Shepherd Rev. A. Henry Powers	Uxbridge/Linwood	10/19/1904
St. Aloysius-St. Jude Rev. Cornelius A. Sullivan	Leicester/Rochdale [8]	11/11/1904
Sacred Heart of Jesus Rev. Rocco Petrarca	Milford	05/08/1905
Our Lady of Mount Carmel Msgr. Gioacchino Maffei	Worcester [2]	11/04/1906
St. Joseph Rev. John P. Phelan	Auburn	01/28/1907
St. Anthony di Padua Rev. Pasquale M. Russomanno	Fitchburg	04/26/1908
Sacred Heart of Jesus Rev. Emile St. Onge	Southbridge	11/15/1908
St. Joseph Rev. Julius Rodziewicz	Gardner	12/06/1908
Our Lady of the Holy Rosary Rev. Edward J. Fitzgerald	Clinton	10/07/1909
Ascension Rev. James E. Farrell	Worcester	07/10/1911
Our Lady of the Rosary Rev. Gedeon Fontaine	Worcester	11/01/1911
Blessed Sacrament Rev. William E. Ryan	Worcester	06/23/1912
St. Stanislaus Rev. Valerian Fligier	(West) Warren	01/ /1913
St. Francis of Assisi Rev. Francis Meskauskas	Athol	05/16/1913
Our Lady of Jasna Gora Rev. Theodore Suk	Clinton [12]	06/17/1913
Immaculate Conception Rev. John F. Boyle	Lancaster	03/26/1915
Our Lady of the Angels Rev. Michael J. O'Connell	Worcester	10/01/1916

Our Lady in St. Leo Church,
Leominster

PARISH	CITY/TOWN	ESTABLISHED
St. Bernard Rev. George F. Flynn	Worcester	11/12/1916
St. Peter Rev. Thomas F. McKoan; Rev. Jules Simoneau, S.S.S.	Petersham [9]	05/02/1917; 05/15/1968
St. Anthony of Padua Rev. Paul Herman	Dudley [5]	06/20/1917
St. Hedwig Rev. Martin S. Hanyz	Southbridge	01/01/1918
St. Thomas-a-Becket Rev. John T. Casey	(South) Barre [12]	08/30/1922
St. Margaret Mary Rev. James T. Hanrahan	Worcester	09/10/1922
St. Mary Rev. Thomas F. McKoan	Shrewsbury	09/10/1922
Our Lady of Mercy (Maronite Rite) Rev. Paul Rissk	Worcester [13]	05/01/1923-01/10/1966
Our Lady of Perpetual Help (Melkite Rite) Rev. Polycarpe N. Warde, B.S.O.	Worcester [13]	01/29/1924-01/10/1966
Our Lady of Vilna Rev. Julius Caplikas	Worcester	05/16/1925
St. Ann Rev. Patrick F. Hafey	(North) Oxford	10/01/1926
St Theresa Rev. Hormidas Remy	(East) Blackstone	07/07/1929
Sacred Heart of Jesus Rev. John H. Donahue	Hopedale	10/26/1935
Christ the King Rev. John F. Reilly	Worcester	07/18/1936
St. Patrick Rev. Martin J. Welsh	Rutland	07/24/1938
St. Anna Rev. John F. Gannon (resident administrator)	Leominster	11/12/1939
Our Lady of Lourdes Rev William F. Ahern	Worcester	01/20/1949
St. Anne Rev. Thomas J. Smith	Shrewsbury	03/29/1950
St. Theresa of the Little Flower Rev. Raymond S. Burke	Harvard [12]	03/29/1950
Sacred Heart of Jesus Rev. Michael E. Shea	West Brookfield	06/01/1950
St. Boniface Rev. John E. O'Toole	Lunenburg	07/05/1950
St. Joan of Arc Rev. John F. Sullivan	Worcester	10/15/1950
St. Edward the Confessor Rev. Thomas J. Connellan	Westminster	06/01/1951
St. Columba Rev. Harry A. Brabson	Paxton	09/05/1951
St. Denis Rev. Joseph A. Lacey	Ashburnham	09/05/1951
St. George Rev. George V. O'Rourke	Worcester	09/05/1951
Our Lady of Fatima Rev. Joseph P. O'Connell	Worcester	01/02/1952
Madonna of the Holy Rosary Rev. Erminio Mastroianni (resident administrator)	Fitchburg	03/22/1952
St. Mary Rev. John A. Finn	(North) Grafton	04/30/1952
Our Lady of the Lake Rev. Francis J. Craven	Leominster/Whalom	07/02/1952

Our Lady in

Holy Spirit Church, Gardner

PARISH	CITY/TOWN	ESTABLISHED
St. Catherine of Sweden Rev. Thomas V. Reilly	Worcester	07/02/1952
St. John the Baptist Rev. Joseph H. Carey	East Brookfield	07/02/1952
St. Michael the Archangel Rev. John J. Foley	Mendon	07/02/1952
St. Mary of the Hills Rev. Harold F. Griffin	Boylston	09/03/1952
Holy Cross Rev. Joseph A. Moynahan	(East) Templeton	09/03/1952
North American Martyrs Rev. Thomas J. O'Rourke	Auburn	10/08/1952
St. Richard of Chichester Rev. Thomas J. Tunney	Sterling	01/14/1953
St. Camillus de Lellis Rev. Edmund P. Marshall	Fitchburg	10/07/1953
St. Francis Xavier Rev. Francis J. Power, (resident administrator)	Bolton	04/16/1954
St. Andrew the Apostle Rev. Thomas J. Carberry	Worcester	11/03/1954
St. Charles Borromeo Rev. Charles M. Bergin	Worcester	11/03/1954
Holy Spirit Rev. John B. O'Connell	Gardner	02/11/1955
Our Lady Queen of Heaven Mission Rev. Aurelius Gariepy, S.S.S., was its founding pastor as a parish,	(South) Royalston	09/ /1955; 01/25/1976 05/15/1968-01/25/1976
St. Vincent de Paul Rev. Arthur J. Heamer	Templeton/Baldwinville	11/06/1955
St. Christopher Rev. Joseph A. Moynahan	Worcester	02/10/1956
St. Pius X Rev. Jeremiah M. Reardon	Leicester	02/24/1956
Prince of Peace Rev. Paul F. Griffin (resident priest-in-charge)	Princeton	09/11/1957
St. Bernadette Rev. Edward F. Kane	Northboro	01/21/1959
St. Andrew Bobola Rev. Casimir A. Swiacki	Dudley	01/15/1963
Holy Family of Nazareth Rev. William J. Harty	Leominster	02/14/1963
Our Lady of Loreto Rev. Joseph A. Porrello	Worcester	09/08/1966
St. Mark Rev. Moise R. Ledoux	Sutton	09/08/1966
St. Joseph the Good Provider Rev. Albin J. Yankauskas	Berlin	08/01/1973
Mary, Queen of the Rosary Rev. James P. Moroney	Spencer[4]	01/01/1994

(1) *St. Anne Mission, along with the Town of Dana, ceased to exist when the Worcester County town and three other Swift River Valley towns in Hampshire County were inundated and removed from the map of the commonwealth in the construction of the Quabbin Reservoir.*

(2) *St. Anne and Our Lady of Mount Carmel Parishes were merged into Our Lady of Mount Carmel — St. Ann (sic) Parish, effective Oct. 1, 1962; St. Anne Church was razed in 1970.*

(3) *Notre Dame des Canadiens and St. Joseph Parishes were merged into Notre Dame des Canadiens-St. Joseph Parish, effective May 31, 1992;*

after extensive consultation it was determined that both churches would still be used.

(4) *Our Lady of the Rosary and St. Mary Parishes, both in Spencer, were suppressed at midnight on Dec. 31, 1993, and immediately Mary, Queen of the Rosary (territorial) Parish was formed from the former territorial/national parishes. Our Lady of the Rosary had been founded in January of 1872 as "St. Mary's"*

Our Lady in
St. Philip Church, Grafton

and assumed its new name in 1883; St. Mary's revived the name of Spencer's original church (and parish) when it was established on Dec. 16, 1886.

(5) In 1968 it was decreed that a new church complex for the the former Slovak parish in Webster would be built in next-door Dudley and that the parish would serve all Slovak people in the Webster-Dudley area as well as all non-Polish-speaking Catholics in Dudley. First Masses were celebrated in Dudley on Dec. 8, 1968, although celebration of Masses continued in the former church in Webster for awhile. The new church in Dudley was dedicated on Oct. 3, 1971.

(6) When 71-year-old St. Anthony Parish, centered in the former Fox Woolen Mills Building in Worcester's inner city, was suppressed, effective Dec. 31, 1975, all of its records and assets were assigned to its mother parish, Notre Dame des Canadiens Parish.

(7) When the Fiskdale parish was founded (1887) as "St. Anne Parish," it had two churches dedicated to St. Anne and St. Patrick — former missions of the so-called "French" and "Irish" parishes in Southbridge. It was named to honor St. Anne, however, because its membership was predominantly French-Canadian and because the popular St. Anne Shrine was located on its grounds. In the early-1950s, however, after the death of Father Joseph Jacques, Father Raymond J. Page, administrator of the parish and later vicar general of the diocese, said, the people determined that since they all used both churches regularly and the communicants of both churches considered themselves to be members of the same parish, "we just began calling ourselves 'St. Anne and St. Patrick Parish'."

(8) A mission of St. Joseph, Leciester, or St. Roch, Oxford, for 35 years, the timbers of the so-called "gypsy church" that gave form to St. Aloysius Church, began their pilgrimage in Grafton in 1846. They were reconfigured as St. Polycarpe's in Leicester center in 1855 and finally were fashioned into the charming St. Aloysius Church in the Rochdale section of Leciester in 1869. The parish established a mission territory in the Dawn Acres section of Leicster in 1957 and in 1965 parishioners completed construction of St. Jude Chapel there. In 1988, when age had taken its toll of the mother church, principal parish Masses began to be celebrated in the Dawn Acres "chapel," with the mother church being designated a "chapel of convenience where the Blessed Sacrament will be reserved." On the Feast of St. Aloysius Gonzaga, June 21, 1995, Worcester's Bishop Daniel P. Reilly renamed the parish "St. Aloysius-St. Jude" to officially recognize reality.

(9) Noted are the two founding years for each of the five parishes; each had parochial stature and was reduced to mission status before being reestablished as a separate parish. (A) St. Bridget's, later known as St. Brigid's, that had been served from St. John's in Worcester, returned to being a mission from 09/20/1853 to 06/30/1869. (B) St. Mary's, Uxbridge, originally served from Milford and Blackstone, returned to being a mission of Blackstone in 1857 when Uxbridge's founding pastor, Rev. Edward J. Sheridan, was named pastor in Blackstone and kept Uxbridge as a mission; a pastor was not named to succeed him in Uxbridge until 1867 when one was also named

to succeed him in Blackstone. (C) Our Lady of Good Counsel, first known as St. Luke's and later as St. Anthony's, assumed its present title in 1903, as far as can be determined, when it was reconstructed in the Oakdale section of town during the inundation for the Wachusett Reservoir of that part of the valley of the Nashua, Quinnepoxet and Stillwater Rivers; it, too, had originally been served from St. John's and returned to mission status from 1905 to 1928. (D) St. Matthew's, in the Cordaville section of Southboro, originally the mother church of Southboro, was given mission status from sometime around 1899 to 08/18/1956. (It is phrased that way because it is not known exactly when Rev. William Finneran, who was appointed pastor of St. Matthew's in November of 1893, built his rectory next to St. Anne's Mission in the center of town and moved into it, making St. Anne's the mother church and reducing St. Matthew's to mission status; it is known, however, that he was still in Cordaville in 1899, thus the use of that date here; Father Finneran remained pastor of the parish, by whichever name, until November of 1902.) (E) St. Peter's in Petersham, established in 1914 originally a mission of Barre and then of Athol, it became a parish in 1917 and returned to mission status in 1933 when four Swift River Valley towns were being readied for inundation in the construction of the Quabbin Reservoir, and remained so until 05/15/1968.

(10) St. Paul's was "raised to the dignity of a cathedral church" on Jan. 14, 1950, in the Papal Brief through which Pope Pius XII announced the erection of the Diocese of Worcester from territory previously part of the Diocese of Springfield.

(11) St. Joseph Church, the church of the first parish for Polish-speaking Catholics in New England, was raised to the dignity of minor basilica on Oct. 11, 1998; at the time it was said to be one of only 36 basilicas in the nation.

(12) The names of several missions/parishes were adapted after the new Diocese of Worcester was established, for example, St. Mary Mission in Boylston became St. Mary of the Hills Parish; St. Teresa of the Child Jesus Mission in Harvard became St. Theresa (and later St. Theresa of the Little Flower) Parish; St. Bridget Parish in Millbury, became St. Brigid Parish, and St. Thomas Parish in South Barre, named to honor St. Thomas the Apostle, the patron saint of Bishop Thomas Beaven, was renamed to honor St. Thomas-a-Becket and through him to recognize the kindness and the generosity of the English-born founder of the Barre Wool Co. who donated the land on which the parish church is built; St. Mary's in Worcester and St. Mary's in Clinton were renamed Our Lady of Czestochowa and Our Lady of Jasna Gora, respectively, to better identify them as Polish-language parishes.

(13) Our Lady of Mercy and Our Lady of Perpetual Help Parishes were attached, respectively, to the (Maronite Rite) Apostolic Exarchate of St. Maron, then centered in Detroit, and the (Melkite Rite) Apostolic Exarchate of Newton, when those jurisdictions were established by Pope Paul VI in early-1966.

Our Lady in
St. Mary Church, Milford

SCHOOLS WITHIN
THE DIOCESE OF WORCESTER*

PARISH ERECTED IN	PARISH/CITY OR TOWN	GRADE SCHOOL OPENS	GRADE SCHOOL CLOSES	HIGH SCHOOL OPENS	HIGH SCHOOL CLOSES
1836	St. John, Worcester	1888[3]	1976[4]	1898	1954[5]
1850	St. Mary, Milford	1880	1975	1925	1974[9]
1850	St. Paul, Blackstone	1928	1971		
1852	St. Louis, Webster	1882		1882	1969
1853	St. Mary, Uxbridge	1964	1976[6]		
1856	St. Bernard, Fitchburg	1886[3]		1927	1960[9]
1856	St. Anne, Worcester[1]	1904	1976[4]	1904	1970[9]
1862	St. John, Clinton	1888	1977[4]		
1865	St. Mary, Southbridge	1889[9]		1894	1965[9]
1866	St. Paul, Worcester	1912	1971		
1867	St. Joseph, North Brookfield	1888	1971		
1869	Notre Dame des Canadiens, Worcester[1]	1881[7]	1957	1941	1942
1869	Notre Dame, Southbridge	1871	1972	1934	1965[9]
1870	Sacred Heart of Jesus, Webster	1885[7]			
1872	St. Leo, Leominster	1926			
1880	Sacred Heart of Jesus, Worcester	1927	1973		
1880	Sacred Heart of Jesus, Gardner	1922			
1880	St. Joseph, Leicester	1914	1979		
1880	Sacred Heart of Jesus, Fitchburg	1890	1970		
1884	Our Lady of the Assumption, Millbury	1925			
1884	St. Peter, Worcester	1921	1971	1922	1976[9]
1884	Our Lady of the Holy Rosary, Gardner	1884			
1886	St. Mary, Spencer[2]	1892	1973		
1886	Immaculate Conception, Fitchburg	1887	1970		
1887	St. Stephen, Worcester	1924		1924	1971[9]
1888	St. Joseph, Webster	1892			
1889	St. Patrick, Whitinsville	1931	1971		
1890	St. Joseph, Fitchburg	1890		1900	1925
1891	St. Joseph, Worcester[1]	1886[7]	1970		
1893	Holy Name of Jesus, Worcester	1885[7]	1977	1942	1957[9]
1893	St. Thomas Aquinas, West Warren	1903	1969		
1894	St. Aloysius, Gilbertville	1889	1970		
1894	St. Casimir, Worcester	1924[8]	1986		
1900	St. Cecilia, Leominster	1901	1977		
1900	St. Anne, Manchaug	1886	1924		
1903	Our Lady of Czestochowa, Worcester	1915		1936	
1903	St. Francis of Assisi, Fitchburg	1904	1971		
1904	St. Anthony, Worcester[2]	1897	1957		
1904	St. Peter, Northbridge	1928	1976		
1904	Good Shepherd, Linwood	1921	1972		
1905	Sacred Heart of Jesus, Milford	1927	1975[6]		
1908	St. Anthony di Padua, Fitchburg	1951			
1908	Sacred Heart of Jesus, Southbridge	1910	1976		
1909	Our Lady of the Holy Rosary, Clinton	1911	1972		
1911	Ascension, Worcester	1872	1963	1872	1970
1912	Blessed Sacrament, Worcester	1926	1974		
1913	Our Lady of Jasna Gora, Clinton	1936[3]			
1916	Our Lady of the Angels, Worcester	1947			
1917	St. Anthony of Padua, Webster/Dudley	1950	1971		
1922	St. Mary, Shrewsbury	1961			
1929	St. Theresa, Blackstone	1929	1974		
1937	St. Anna, Leominster	1953			
1959	St. Bernadette, Northboro	1997			

NOTES	PRIVATE OR DIOCESAN SCHOOL/CITY OR TOWN	GRADE SCHOOL OPENS	GRADE SCHOOL CLOSES	HIGH SCHOOL OPENS	HIGH SCHOOL CLOSES
	Assumption Prep School, Worcester			1904	1970
	Holy Cross Prep School, Worcester[11]			1843	1914
	Holy Family Schools, Fitchburg	1957	1987	1962	1978
	Holy Name C.C. High School			1957[9]	
	Immaculate Heart of Mary, Still River	1958		1958	
	Julie Country Day School, Leominster	1941			
	Maria Assumpta Academy, Petersham			1951	1973
	Marianhill/Trinity C.C.H.S., Southbridge			1965[9]	1990
	Mercy Centre, Worcester	1961			
	Milford Central Catholic School, Milford	1975			
	Mount St. James Academy, Worcester[11]	1838	1843	1838	1843
	Mount St. Joseph Industrial, Millbury	1900	1915	1900	1915
	Notre Dame Academy, Worcester			1951	
	Notre Dame High School, Fitchburg			1951	
	Our Lady of the Valley School, Uxbridge	1976			
	St. Bernard C.C. High School			1960[9]	
	St. John High School, Shrewsbury			1954	
	St. Peter Central Elementary, Worcester[10]	1976			
	St. Peter-Marian C.C.H.S., Worcester			1963[9]	
	Trivium School, Lancaster			1979	
	Venerini Academy, Worcester	1945		1945	1970

*   Christ the King Parish, Worcester (1936), conducted an exclusively-pre-primary school from 1949 to 1968, as did Our Lady Immaculate Parish, Athol (1882), from 1946 to 1967. St. Anne Orphanage for boys and girls (1889-1979) and St. Gabriel Orphanage for girls (1875-1955), both in Worcester, and Nazareth Home for boys in Leicester that opened in 1901 and still functions, had classrooms within their walls, but also sent pupils to neighboring parochial or public schools.

(1) Parish now hyphenated (merged).

(2) Parish now suppressed.

(3) Date indicates beginning of continuous operation of school, following earlier openings and closings.

(4) School closed after attempts at merger also failed.

(5) School now a non-parish, private Catholic institution.

(6) School now operating as a regional elementary school.

(7) For a time, these schools also had a two-year commercial course for high school-age youngsters.

(8) From 1937 to 1958 St. Casimir's also had a freshman year of high school.

(9) St. Peter's High was merged with Marian High, founded in 1963 as an all-girls diocesan school, in 1976 to form St. Peter-Marian High, a diocesan central school, on the Marian campus. In 1967, 10 years after it was classified as a central Catholic high school, rather than a parish high school, Holy Name High moved onto a new campus on Granite Street, far from its native parish, but just across the street from St. Anne Orphanage, whose roots were entwined with those of the Holy Name Schools. St. Bernard's went from parish to diocesan sponsorship in 1960. Notre Dame High and St. Mary High, both in Southbridge, merged into Marianhill High School, a diocesan-sponsored central Catholic school in 1965; it, in turn (1988) became part of Trinity Catholic Academy, but in 1990 the high school section closed. St. Mary Elementary School, Southbridge, also was regionalized as part of Trinity Academy in 1988, but early in 2000 it reverted to parochial status. St. Mary High, Milford, and St. Stephen High and Ascension High, both in Worcester, and the high school section of Sacred Heart Academy (St. Anne Parish), Worcester, had all ceased to be parish-sponsored high schools and were part of the central Catholic school system before their closing.

(10) What was originally known as Worcester Central Catholic Elementary School had its beginnings in 1963 with the merger of St. John and Ascension Schools. In 1976, following other mergers, the central, diocesan-sponsored elementary school consolidated all its classes in the former buildings of St. Peter Parish Schools on Main Street. It took its present name in 1996.

(11) The secondary school section of Father James Fitton's Mount St. James Academy, became part of what evolved into Holy Cross College after Jesuit Fathers assumed its direction in 1843. In June of 1914 the last of the preparatory school grades was terminated and Holy Cross became a four-year, degree-granting college exclusively.

Our Lady in Immaculate Conception Church, Worcester